seventeen
ULTIMATE GUIDE TO
BEAUTY

SEVENTEEN ULTIMATE GUIDE TO BEAUTY

Published by Running Press,
A Member of the Perseus Books Group

Printed in China

Books published by Running Press are available at special discounts
for bulk purchases in the United States by corporations,
institutions, and other organizations. For more information, please
contact the Special Markets Department at the Perseus Books Group,
2300 Chestnut Street, Suite 200, Philadelphia, PA 19103, or
call (800) 810-4145, ext. 5000, or e-mail special.markets@perseusbooks.com.

ISBN: 978-0-7624-4524-0
Library of Congress Control Number: 2012935723

E-book ISBN: 978-0-7624-4543-1

9 8 7 6 5 4 3 2
Number on the right indicates the number of this printing

Running Press Book Publishers
2300 Chestnut Street
Philadelphia, PA 19103-4371
Visit us on the web! www.runningpress.com

seventeen
ULTIMATE GUIDE TO
BEAUTY
THE BEST HAIR, SKIN, NAILS & MAKEUP IDEAS FOR YOU

ANN SHOKET
& THE EDITORS *of seventeen*

Editor
JOANNA SALTZ

Beauty Director
YESENIA ALMONTE

PUBLISHED
by

RUNNING PRESS
PHILADELPHIA · LONDON

PRODUCED
by

Hi from Ann!

The *Seventeen* beauty closet is **total girl heaven**! It's filled floor to ceiling with every single beauty product imaginable: gorgeous new **eyeshadow** palettes, amazing **mascaras,** lush **lipsticks,** a rainbow of **liners,** fun lip **glosses,** and tons of products that promise long, shiny, perfect hair! (You can often catch me in there late on a Friday evening picking out a new shade of polish for my weekend mani.)

I love a great **beauty haul**! But what happens when you get those new products home? What are you supposed to do with that new smoky-eye kit? How do you get that intricate fishtail braid you saw online? Let's be honest: Beauty can be sort of intimidating.

That's where *Seventeen* comes in. It's our mission to give you **total beauty confidence**! We'll help you find your **personal makeup vibe,** then walk you through the **hottest new looks,** step-by-step. And when it comes to hair, no one is more obsessed than we are—there are dozens of the best looks for every hair texture inside. To take it one step further: We've **customized** each chapter for *your* life, so you can rock these ideas anywhere—at school, on the weekend, on a date, or to a party!

This book is also jammed with amazing secrets from the top industry pros. But even more importantly, we are highlighting our **real-girl beauty experts, *Seventeen*'s Beauty Smarties.** They are just regular girls who love hair and makeup so much that they want to share their best tricks with the world—their beauty how-to videos on YouTube have millions of views! Here, they create new looks just for you.

With our team of editors and experts on your side, you'll never be intimidated again. Because whether you're a hair and makeup newbie or a total product junkie, this book celebrates your **true beauty.**

XOXO
-A.

YOUR ULTIMATE

makeup guide

SHIMMERY LIPSTICK

Soft shades of pearl, lilac, pink, and honey come to life with **sparkly highlights.**

LAVENDER SHADOW

Brush onto lids for a **fresh, flirty look.**

BLUSH/BRONZER COMBO

A **rosy blush** on your apples plus a **bronzer** below your cheekbones equals a gorgeous glow!

girly

The perfect girly look mixes sweet, romantic colors with refined touches for pop and polish. Try ultra-feminine lips with thickly lashed eyes. Or play with sheer textures and dress them up with a little sparkle. You'll get a look that's equally cute *and* cool.

ULTIMATE *girly* LOOKS

These four feminine looks will take you anywhere!

17 TIP:
Dab concealer onto your eyelids before you apply shadow to prevent fading and smudging.

STEP 1:
Create major impact by applying **bold shades** with a soft touch. Sweep them on with a fluffy brush—the looser bristles make for a lighter application.

STEP 2:
Add a **pink cream blush** to the apples of cheeks—the lightweight texture gives you a dewy flush.

STEP 3:
For a pretty finish, swipe on a **sheer pink gloss.** It'll balance out your bright eyes in a daytime-friendly way.

school

Amp up your signature pink cheeks and lips by pairing them with an unexpected eye combo!

STEP 1:

Try wearing **silver cream shadow** as eyeliner—a thin streak at the base of your lashes can make a big impact.

STEP 2:

Put on a super-long pair of **fake lashes,** then coat your top and bottom lashes with mascara for a wide-eyed effect.

STEP 3:

For cheeks that pop, sweep a **tawny blush** just below your cheekbones.

party

Light up the night with a mix of subtle-yet-sexy textures (and just a touch of glitter).

STEP 1:
Create a porcelain palette with **liquid foundation**—the extra coverage makes makeup colors stand out more.

STEP 2:
Bust out **coppery metallic eyeshadows** for nighttime—they reflect light in the prettiest way.

STEP 3:
A **glittery berry gloss** is bold and brightens your whole complexion—skip the blush to avoid color overload.

date

A fresh fuchsia lip is just right for a night out with your crush—it makes your pout irresistible.

STEP 1:

A wash of **opalescent cream shadow** on your top lids brightens your whole face and is so easy to smudge on with fingers!

STEP 2:

A **multicolored blush**—with tiny flecks of gold—gives you a healthy glow. Swirl it onto the apples of your cheeks and then sweep it up to your temples.

STEP 3:

Give your lips a natural look with a pop of shine— dab on a **nude gloss** with a touch of pearlescence.

weekend

It doesn't take a ton of effort to look this pretty—a few hints of shimmer make you look lit from within.

TOP *girly* SECRETS

Try these tricks from Hollywood's top makeup artists!

1 GET A ROSY GLOW!

"Blend a dot of your lipstick onto your cheeks. The warmth of your skin makes the color go on more like a stain, creating a subtly rosy look." –**Gita Bass**

Kendall Jenner

2 OPEN UP YOUR EYES!

"Line the inner rims of your eyes with shimmery vanilla-colored liner. It's not as harsh as white, but it'll still make eyes look bigger and more awake." –**Mario Dedivanovic**

Keke Palmer

Chloë Grace Moretz

3

PLAY UP YOUR CHEEKBONES!

"Use a highlighter right above the cheekbone, near the eye area, to add dimension to your face. Go with a shade that's close to your skin tone. If your skin is pale, try champagne or silver highlighter. Gold looks best on medium or tan complexions. And if you're dark, go for bronze. You'll look lit from within!" –Mai Quynh

Lauren Conrad

5

GET KISSED WITH COLOR!

"To keep pink blush from looking too sweet, pair it with a berry lipstick." –Coleen Campbell-Olwell

Lily Collins

4

SOFTEN SMOKY EYES!

"The key is taking a light version and a dark version of a color and blending them together. I love this technique with coppers, blues, greens, and purples." –Amy Nadine

seventeen
BEAUTY SMARTIES

Alexis

AGE: 21

HOMETOWN: Astoria, NY

STAR SIGN: Scorpio

FAVE COLOR: Pink

HOBBIES: Dancing, reading, shopping

" **I love soft colors like lilac, pink, and peach. They make me feel girly and pretty.** "

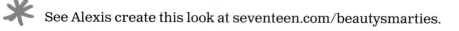 See Alexis create this look at seventeen.com/beautysmarties.

MY BEAUTY ICON

"**Chanel Iman.** She can get glammed up or she can look girly, fun, and young—an all-around versatile girl."

FASHION OBSESSION

"I love **bracelets** and bangles. They dress up any outfit!"

FAVORITE TREND

"**Red lips.** Red looks great on everyone!"

my ♥ inspirations

MY GO-TO LOOK

"**Shimmery eyeshadow.** It adds pop and brings the focus to my eyes."

MY ESSENTIAL TOOL

"**A kabuki brush.** The short bristles blend everything—liquid or powder makeup—and it's small enough to carry around with me."

MY CELEB CRUSH

"**Zoe Saldana.** I loved her first movie, *Center Stage*—I am also a dancer! I thought her delicate look was so pretty."

MY FAVORITE FLOWER

"**Asiatic lilies,** specifically the pink ones—my favorite color. I received a bunch for my birthday last year, and I've been in love with them ever since."

Alexis's look:
LAVENDER SMOKE

"This look is flirty and sexy, but not *too* sexy! The pink gives it a sweet touch."

" Purple is such a fun eyeshadow shade, and it really makes my eye color pop."

HOW-TO:

SWIPE

" Blend **plum shadow** from the base of lashes to just above the creases of your lids, then swipe a bit underneath bottom lashes for a delicate wash of color. Finish with liner and mascara for definition."

DAB

" A **cream blush** or **liquid stain** gives the softest flush. Dab it onto the apples of your cheeks and blend in small, circular motions."

APPLY

" **Shiny pink gloss** is the perfect finishing touch. A sponge-tip applicator is great for applying a generous amount; a brush is better if you want more control."

" I like to put a little bit of shimmer under the arch of my brows to make my eyes stand out more."

" Pink glosses are great because they go with practically everything."

" I prefer a pencil liner because it goes on softer than liquid. And if I mess up, it's easier to fix."

21

YOUR *girly* LOOK BOOK

TAYLOR SWIFT

Statement-making fuchsia lips stand out on their own! Keep the rest of your makeup light for a romantic feel.

KAT GRAHAM

Pair lush lashes with strong eyebrows. Fill them in with a brow pencil, then brush through the hairs to blend.

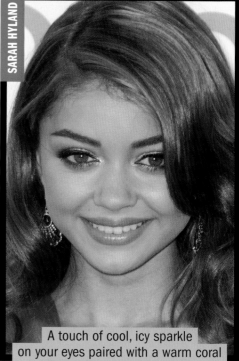

SARAH HYLAND

A touch of cool, icy sparkle on your eyes paired with a warm coral lip makes for one hot look!

NINA RICCI

Mattify any lipstick color! Blot the color with a tissue, then lightly dust a translucent powder over your lips.

LEIGHTON MEESTER

A shot of gloss to just the center of lips makes your lips extrapouty.

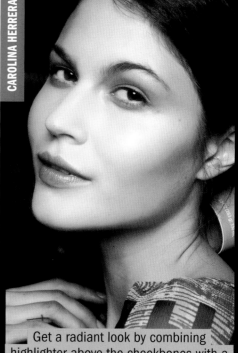

CAROLINA HERRERA

Get a radiant look by combining highlighter above the cheekbones with a contouring sweep of bronzer below them.

Get inspired by these celeb and runway looks—the makeup possibilities are endless!

NINA RICCI

Make your lips look extraflirty with a dab of light shimmer on your Cupid's bow.

JENNA USHKOWITZ

Yes, you can get away with barely there makeup at night. Balance out nude lips and cheeks with smudgy, neutral eyeshadow.

PAUL & JOE

For a doe-eyed effect, pair fluttery lashes with a swipe of shimmery shadow just on the inner corners of your eyes.

EMMA ROBERTS

Even with a nude face and lip, winged black eyeliner is super-flirty!

CAROLINA HERRERA

For a sweet flush, apply a creamy pink blush *only* on the apples.

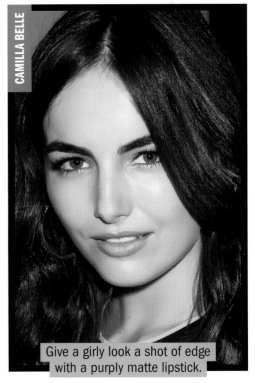

CAMILLA BELLE

Give a girly look a shot of edge with a purply matte lipstick.

23

GOLD HIGHLIGHTER

Glide a gleaming pencil over lips, eyes, or cheekbones to create a **light-catching glow.**

MULTICOLORED SHADOW

Swirl your brush over these shades, then sweep onto lids for a **dimensional look.**

SMOKY-EYE PALETTE

A deep, sexy eye is your signature look. A bit of jewel-toned shadow keeps it **fresh**!

glam

Glam girls know how to get noticed. Whether it's a bold stroke of lip color, look-at-me lashes, or a burst of eye-catching sparkle, your approach to makeup is a little bit flashy and always fearless.

ULTIMATE glam LOOKS

These four fierce looks will take you anywhere!

STEP 1:
For a **simple yet sultry** look, paint an elongated line across your top lids and go halfway on bottom.

STEP 2:
One coat of volumizing mascara on top and bottom lashes makes your eyes *and* liner pop!

STEP 3:
A light dusting of translucent powder keeps your skin from getting *too* dewy.

school

Look chic during the week—a super-dramatic wing is bound to catch everyone's eye.

STEP 2:

Dust your eyes with **golden glimmer**—it's subtle enough to blend all the way up to your eyebrows.

STEP 1:

For a lit-from-within glow, rub **gold-flecked liquid bronzer** onto the apples of your cheeks and blend well.

17 TIP:
Don't have gold shadow? Rub a little bronzer onto your lids to light up your eyes.

weekend

When you keep them monochromatic and neutral, allover metallics add just enough flash for a dressed-down day.

STEP 3:

Swipe on **gleaming lip gloss** for an instantly luscious pout.

STEP 1:
Budgeproof **gel liner** is perfect for date night! Pull your lid taut, then trace it along your top lashline with a tapered brush.

STEP 2:
For a playful look, layer **metallic blue liner** on top of the black on just the center of lids.

STEP 3:
Peachy cheek **and lip stain** looks so fresh with dolled-up eyes!

date

Strategically placed sparkles are a sophisticated way to show off your wild side.

STEP 1:

Perfect your brows with a **soft pencil.** Use gentle strokes along your natural arch.

STEP 2:

For eyes that have lasting gleam, apply **shimmery shadow** over a neutral matte shade.

STEP 3:

Black pencil liner on upper and lower lash-lines defines your eye shape and sets off shadow beautifully.

party

Hit the town with luminous lids
that catch the light just right!

TOP glam SECRETS

Try these tricks from Hollywood's top makeup artists!

1 BRING ON THE DRAMA!

" For extra intensity around the eyes, apply mascara to your bottom lashes. I like to pat a flat, square liner brush onto the wand, then brush it on the lashes. It gives me more control, and less product gets onto the brush, so it's easier to layer on a lot of coats."
–Mai Quynh

Ashley Benson

Bella Thorne

2 TRY METALLIC LIDS!

" To add zing to your usual makeup look, take a shimmery silver or pewter shadow and apply it with a damp brush. When you apply it wet, it dries to a glazed finish that looks like cream shadow but lasts longer." **–Brett Freedman**

4 GET CHIC FAST!

"To get glam fast, try a bold lip—that instantly takes it up a notch! If you're going with a bright shade like red or fuchsia, fill in lips with a matching lip pencil first. It helps the color last longer and defines the lip."
–Mylah Morales

Leighton Meester

Amber Riley

3 PLAY WITH TEXTURE!

"A soft, nude lipstick can make you look striking without zapping your glow—you can opt for subtle glam with a matte version or really gloss it up for high shine." **–Brett Freedman**

Jenna Ushkowitz

5 GET GLOSSY!

"Gloss on the lids gives you a glam, super-shiny look—but pick a nude or peach shade to help it feel neutral."
–Charlotte Willer

seventeen
BEAUTY
SMARTIES

Bianca

AGE: 22

HOMETOWN: San Jose, CA

STAR SIGN: Scorpio

FAVE COLOR: Pink

HOBBIES: Cooking, reading, watching scary movies

" **I'm constantly changing my look, but it's always bold. I'm not afraid to be different—I love to stand out.** "

 See Bianca create this look at seventeen.com/beautysmarties.

MY GET-NOTICED TRICK

" Wear **super-bright lipstick.** A lot of girls like to play up their eyes at night, so when you go out with bold lipstick, you get more attention."

ME IN ACTION

" I truly enjoy doing makeup on others. I love **making people happy** with makeup."

MY FAVORITE ACCESSORY

" I'm really into **big gold jewelry.** It makes me feel glamorous."

my inspirations

MY BEAUTY WEAKNESS

"**Nail polish**! I can never have enough. I always buy the newest colors every season."

MY GOING-OUT LOOK

" I have a **cute black sequined jacket** that's perfect over a cami and jeans. I wear it with **patent leather pumps.**"

MY CELEB CRUSH

" **Beyoncé**'s makeup is always flawless. I love the dramatic way she accentuates her eyes in her 'Countdown' music video—here's a version I did in a beauty video."

33

Bianca's look: LAVISH LASHES

"I wear fake lashes almost every day. I don't feel complete until they're on!"

" Lining the inner rims of your eyes ups the intensity level and adds extra definition—it's a must-do step for me."

HOW-TO:

SWEEP

" **Frosty gold shadow** is a great base for dramatic lashes—they'll stand out more. Dust it just above the creases of your eyes, and put some in the inner corners for extra pop."

PLACE

" Fake bigger, brighter eyes with a pair of **faux lashes.** Look down into a mirror to help place them properly. They should sit right on top of your lashline."

DEFINE

" For a polished, 'done' look, give your brows a boost with **brown powder.** Stroke on the color with a stiff, angled brush, then smudge the hairs with your fingers to blend."

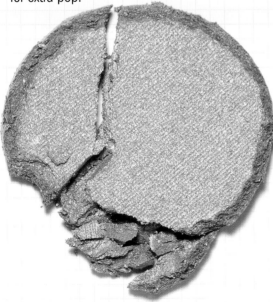

" If you want extra color, use a flat brush and *press* the powder onto your lids instead of brushing it— you'll get more pigment."

" I'm always changing the style of my lashes. During the day, I go for a more natural look. At night, I bust out crazier ones."

" Pink lips go well with gold eyes. You just need that little pop of color."

35

YOUR glam LOOK BOOK

EMMA STONE

A crazy-bold pink lipstick will get you going-out-ready fast! Make it last with two coats of color.

DIANNA AGRON

Experiment with a graphic eye—a smudged blue line that's close to the eye looks fun and sophisticated.

RIHANNA

Coppery lids and bronze cheeks are a gorgeous combo on every skin tone!

NIKKI REED

Red lips look ultra-sexy with strong brows and flushed cheeks.

JORDIN SPARKS

Rich, chocolaty tones on eyes and lips are a fresh take on the smoky eye/nude lip combo.

TORY BURCH

Smoldering eyes are a foolproof after-dark statement. Prep your lids with loose powder first to keep shadow from smearing.

Get inspired by these celeb and runway looks— the makeup possibilities are endless!

LUCY HALE

Long, thick lashes always look hot. To turn up the intensity, trace the insides of your lashlines with a black pencil.

KAT GRAHAM

A true glam girl doesn't shy away from glitter. Dust it on just the inside corners of your eyes so you don't look costumey.

RALPH LAUREN

One guaranteed way to get noticed: Rock retro red lipstick.

KATY PERRY

Pastel eyeshadow is unexpected and fresh at night. Feeling daring? Try a contrasting shade along lashlines.

HEATHER MORRIS

Fake a fuller pout with a layer of frosty gloss applied to the center of your top and bottom lips—slick it over lipstick for sexy shine.

JASON WU

Take a break from the pink-blush path and try a pop of coral or peach instead.

SHEER FOUNDATION

The **light texture** creates a sheer, smooth canvas!

RED LIPSTICK

The **right red** never fails to flatter! If your skin tone is medium to dark, opt for an orangy red; if you're fair, then a blue-red will flatter your skin.

ROSY PINK BLUSH

Gives you a **sheer wash of color** so you look naturally flushed.

NEUTRAL LIP PENCIL

When your eyes are the focus, a neutral lip strikes the right note, **defined yet natural**.

classic

Classic girls love timeless makeup—but they're not afraid to add a modern twist! Think fresh updates like red gloss, navy fluttery lashes, or shimmery lids. It's not about playing it safe—it's about knowing what works for you, then making it your own. You'll get a gorgeous look that never goes out of style.

BLACK LIQUID LINER

Paints the **perfect cat-eye** with just one stroke!

PEARLY SHADOW STICK

Luminescent and creamy, it lights up your eyes!

ULTIMATE classic LOOKS

These four pretty looks will take you anywhere!

STEP 3:
To let your eyes take center stage, go for a **soft pink** on your lips.

STEP 1:
Make your eyes look instantly bigger and brighter—smudge a **sparkly gold** all over lids and onto the inner "v" of your eyes.

STEP 2:
Apply three coats of the **blackest black volumizing mascara** to pop against the gold shimmer on your eyes.

party

A few dramatic details—a touch of mega-metallic shadow, super-long lashes—make an understated look totally unforgettable.

STEP 1:
The pointy tip of a **liquid liner pen** will give a neat, precise line. Start by tracing it thinly along the base of your top lashes, then build it up if you want a thicker effect.

STEP 2:
A **mauvy cheek color** balances bright lips so you don't look like you're wearing tons of makeup.

STEP 3:
A **bright, sheer gloss** gives you a juicy pop of color in an understated way.

school

Black liner and red lips is a tried-and-true Hollywood look—but a neat wing and sheer gloss tone it down for class.

STEP 2:
For radiant eyes, sweep an iridescent **vanilla-colored shadow** across your top lids.

STEP 1:
Even out your skin tone in a natural-looking way with a **sheer liquid foundation.** Use it only where you need it—like around your nose or under your eyes.

STEP 3:
A **matte petal shade** gives a light color that looks like your natural lips.

17 TIP:
Use a single coat of curling mascara! With makeup this light, soft lashes become part of the pretty, un-made-up effect.

weekend

A nearly naked palette has that effortless, I-look-this-good-all-the-time vibe!

STEP 1:

A layer of **face primer** keeps your skin fresh and shine-free for hours!

STEP 2:

For skin that looks perfectly polished, use a puff to apply a **light-coverage translucent powder** over your primer.

STEP 3:

Feel extraconfident and flirty with a bright burst of **orangy-red lipstick.**

date

Show off the playful side of your personality— bright lips and a clean face look chic but not overdone.

TOP classic SECRETS

Try these tricks from Hollywood's top makeup artists!

Taylor Swift

1 FAKE FLUTTERY LASHES!

"To get a wispy, natural effect, go with individual lashes instead of a full strip. You can use them to enhance your natural eye shape. If your eyes are round, apply some lashes to the center of your lashline to make them look more almond. If your eyes are smaller, stick lashes on the outer corners to open them up." –**Lusine Galadjian**

2 BRIGHTEN UP!

"On those days when your skin looks dull and pasty, brighten up your whole face by applying icy lavender shadow around your inner tear ducts." –**Tania Saylor**

Selena Gomez

3 REMIX RED LIPS!

"Pick your favorite red shade and mix it with gloss. The sheerer the color, the more youthful the look. For daytime, mix it with a little bit of lip balm so it's not too shiny." –Lusine Galadjian

Victoria Justice

4 MULTITASK YOUR MAKEUP!

"Lipstick and tinted lip balms become great cream blushes in a pinch! Same goes for the reverse—cream blushes can substitute for lip color."
–Amy Nadine

Amanda Seyfried

5 DEFINE YOUR CHEEKS!

Zendaya

"For a romantic flush, smile big and apply a powder or cream blush on the apples. Whether you use a brush or your fingers, make circular motions as you apply to get a perfect flush!" –Amy Nadine

seventeen
BEAUTY SMARTIES

Caitlin

AGE: 17

HOMETOWN: Plymouth, MN

STAR SIGN: Aquarius

FAVE COLOR: Coral

HOBBIES: Playing guitar, making art, spending time with friends, and, of course, making beauty videos!

" I like to keep my look natural but with a pop of something interesting. "

 See Caitlin create this look at seventeen.com/beautysmarties.

BADGLEY MISCHKA

MY INSPIRATIONS

" I love the **jewel-toned fabrics** I see on the runway. They have inspired me to incorporate those colors into my eyeshadows— but in a subtle way so it's not too crazy!"

MY CELEB CRUSH

" **Natalie Portman.** Her skin always looks amazing, like she's glowing from within!"

my inspirations

MY BEAUTY ICON

" **Kate Middleton**! She's absolutely stunning. She always looks put together, and even did her own makeup for her royal wedding. How cool is that?!"

MY FAVORITE CITY

" **Paris**! The architecture is beautiful, and the people are my walking style inspirations."

MY GO-TO LOOK

" I adore a **winged liner, glowy cheeks, and a pink lip.** It's wearable and easy to accomplish when I'm on the go but want to look put together!"

MY PRIZED POSSESSION

" **My gold locket necklace.** It was my grandma's, who passed away, and we were very close! She wore it every day and kept photos of her sisters in it."

Caitlin's look:
RED ROMANCE

"This look is elegant, yet fresh and exciting!"

"Red lipstick seems scary, but it's actually really easy to wear. I love that it makes my teeth look whiter!"

HOW-TO:

BRUSH

"Use a brush to apply vanilla-colored shadow. I like to wear **subtle eyeshadow** with bright lips so that my face looks finished. **Off-white** works great because it doesn't compete with the red."

DUST

"Add warmth to the face with a **sheer blush**—it gives a classic red-lip look a more modern, fresh feel and keeps you from looking washed out."

SWIPE

"**Fire-engine reds** are just so feminine and iconic. It's fine to apply lipstick straight from the tube. Use the tip of the bullet to outline your lips first, then fill them in with color."

"When you're wearing a shimmery eyeshadow, balance it out with matte blush and creamy lipstick so you're not sparkling *everywhere*."

"I always wear blush to offset bold red lips. I just dust on a little bit less so that it doesn't steal the focus away from the red lips."

YOUR classic LOOK BOOK

FREIDA PINTO

A pink palette for cheeks and lips is surprisingly sophisticated when you stick with shimmer-free textures.

DEREK LAM

Create the perfect backdrop for color by covering up skin imperfections with concealer.

LILY COLLINS

Dress up neutral shadow with a smudge of shimmer on the inner corners of your eyes—it's chic and fast!

MICHAEL KORS

Taupe lids and beige lipstick are a simple but sophisticated makeup combo.

NAYA RIVERA

Amp up the drama on your brows and lashes! Keep the face clean, fill in brows in with a pencil, and do three coats of mascara on top lashes.

CHRISTIAN DIOR

Like red, magenta on your lips is versatile enough to wear anywhere if you keep the rest of your face neutral.

Get inspired by these celeb and runway looks— the makeup possibilities are endless!

CHLOË GRACE MORETZ

To toughen up a pretty look, apply black eyeliner on outer corners of top and bottom lashes.

SELENA GOMEZ

Perfectly groomed brows give off a polished, pulled-together vibe. Don't forget to pluck!

DOLCE & GABBANA

A warm pink lip looks elegant and shows you do have a girly side!

EMMA STONE

Pale matte lips are always beautiful, but to add a dose of fun, pair them with shimmery eyes.

KEKE PALMER

The smoky eyes and nude lip look will never go out of style! Balance out the two opposite tones with a sweep of bronzy color on cheeks.

PHILOSOPHY BY ALBERTA FERRETTI

Baby-doll lashes plus pale pink lips are a pretty, timeless combo that will turn heads.

BOLD LASHES

Create a special effect that makes your eyes really **stand out**!

ELECTRIC EYESHADOWS

High-voltage shades give a **mega-dose of color**—use them all over lids or as liner.

FUCHSIA GLOSS

This high-impact shade instantly **energizes your face.**

BLACK GEL LINER

The formula goes on like ink to give you **major drama.**

BRIGHT EYE PENCIL

Trace your eyes with this **vivid color** for a cool-girl effect!

EDGY

Get the edgy look by embracing elements that are strong, daring, and undeniably cool. It could be as easy as adding a swipe of crazy-bright liner or wearing neon lipstick with gunmetal shadow. Just be sure to contrast striking touches with a bit of softness to create an interesting mix that'll keep all eyes on you.

FACE CRYSTALS

Provides **sparkle and impact** to any makeup look!

GUNMETAL EYESHADOW

So **dramatic** with just a coat of mascara.

ULTIMATE EDGY LOOKS

These four cool looks will take you anywhere!

STEP 1:
The weekend is your chance to experiment with makeup. Try a **thin line** on your eye first, then **add another line** next to it. Repeat until you have the thickness you want.

17 TIP:
Amp up your arches with brow pencil or powder—it helps them hold their own against graphic liner.

STEP 2:
For a hint of pink that won't clash with your eyes, opt for a **shimmer-free powder** blush.

STEP 3:
Add a bit of sweetness to your whole look with a **sheer bubble gum lip color**!

WEEKEND

Balance is key when taking an edgy look out during the day—a bold eye needs to be offset by a super-muted lip.

STEP 1:
Look like you spent the weekend outside by rubbing a **luminous cream bronzer** onto the apples of your cheeks, forehead, and along your nose and chin.

STEP 2:
Line your top lids with a **blue pencil** to bring out the color of your lashes even more.

STEP 3:
It doesn't take a lot of effort to rock colorful lashes with **electric blue mascara**! Don't forget to de-clump with a lash comb.

STEP 4:
Look pretty but casual with a natural shade of **nude lipstick** with a creamy texture.

SCHOOL

Your friends wouldn't recognize you without some sort of edgy touch. But sometimes one punch is all you need.

STEP 2:
Cause a stir at any party with **flashy fake lashes.** Trim them to fit your eyes, then practice positioning them before you secure them with lash glue.

STEP 3:
To help your real lashes blend in, do one coat of **black mascara** before *and* after you stick on your falsies.

STEP 1:
Silvery cream eyeshadow is so fresh at night. Blend across lids, then add extra pop with a swipe of vivid blue on the outer corners of your eyes.

PARTY

A night out is the perfect time to shine! Express your creative side with shimmer and drama.

STEP 1:

Get a glowing complexion with a **tinted moisturizer** applied all over your face. Blend outward with fingertips for the most perfect finish.

STEP 2:

For the most unshy eyes, apply a richly pigmented **powder eyeshadow.** Sweep the darker tone along lashlines and in the creases. Fill in your lid and browbone with the paler shade.

STEP 3:

Bring on the tough-girl vibe by applying **jet-black liner** to the insides of your lashlines.

DATE

A smoky eye says you're totally confident—but the pale green color says you're mysterious, too.

TOP EDGY SECRETS

Try these tricks from Hollywood's top makeup artists!

Demi Lovato

1 TOUGHEN UP YOUR SHADOW!

"To make softer eyeshadow shades like plum or gray look edgy, just trace black liner along your upper and lower lashlines and apply it to the inside lashline. Finish with tons of mascara." –Lusine Galadjian

2 CLEAN UP SMUDGES!

"To fix liquid liner gone awry, dip a pointed cotton swab into a bit of body lotion and erase the mistake with a quick drag and wipe. Oily eye-makeup remover can create a canvas that's too greasy for the new line to adhere to." –Amy Nadine

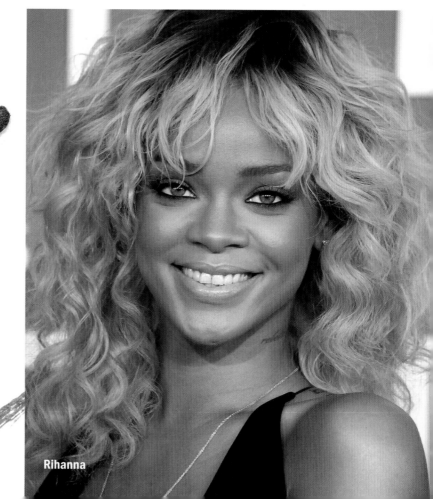

Rihanna

3

GET RID OF CLUMPS!

"To separate clumpy lashes, use a lash comb right after you apply mascara. If you wait until the mascara is dry, it will start flaking and will flake throughout the day."
–Mai Quynh

Katy Perry

Nicki Minaj

4

ROCK DARK LIPS!

"Deep lipsticks look the prettiest with clean, natural-looking skin, curled lashes, and mascara. Dark colors can look too vampy and Halloween-ish if you do too much to the rest of your face." –Mario Dedivanovic

Crystal Reed

5

MASTER FALSE LASHES!

"Before you apply a full strip of fake lashes, measure them against your eye and cut the ends if they're too long. Apply them as close as possible to your lashline. If you're working with individual clusters, dab glue on the ends and stick them on with tweezers." –Mylah Morales

MICHELLE

AGE: 24

HOMETOWN: Tampa, FL

STAR SIGN: Aries

FAVE COLOR: White

HOBBIES: Traveling, drawing

FYI: Michelle Phan, who has been a *Seventeen* Beauty Smartie since the launch in 2009, has become the most popular video makeup artist on YouTube, with more than 500 million views! She's also become the official video makeup artist for prestigious beauty brand Lancôme.

> **I've been painting since I was a little girl, and that's how I approach my work. I love to create dramatic makeup that looks like art.**

✳ See Michelle create this look at seventeen.com/beautysmarties.

MY CELEB CRUSH

"**Gwen Stefani,** hands down. I love her signature red lips and her bold sharp liquid liner. She looks edgy but timeless."

MY FAVORITE MAKEUP TRICK

"Fix a **broken lipstick** by fusing it together with a lighter. It reminds me of making candles when I was younger. It's foolproof!"

MY TOP MUST-HAVE

"**Powder.** A greasy face is never hot."

my inspirations

A TREND I LOVE

"**Bleached brows** were always something that I thought was uniquely beautiful."

MY BEAUTY OBSESSION

"**Volumizing mascara**! This is like false lashes in a tube."

MICHELLE'S LOOK: GALACTIC EYES

"This is the futuristic makeup that Lady Gaga would wear on a first date!"

" The intense gray color adds drama, but it's not as harsh as a jet-black."

HOW-TO:

TRACE

" Draw the shape with a **nude pencil** to create a guide for where the eyeshadow should go. It'll help create an even, defined line."

PREP

" Place **tape along the edges** of the guide before you start applying the shadow. That way you won't have to worry about making a mess."

SHADE

" Fill in the square shape with **charcoal shadow,** leaving a space below the outer corners of your brows. To accent the dark color, fill in the bare skin with a **shimmery soft purple shadow.**"

DEFINE

" To create the illusion of depth and dimension, apply a **black pencil** to the creases of your eyes on top of the dark shadow."

DRAW

" **Little starbursts** are key to the outer-space vibe. Draw them near the outer corners of your eyes with **white shadow** and a tiny brush."

SMUDGE

" Remove the tape. If the edges of the shadow are too sharp, just **soften up the lines** by gently going over them with a brush."

" To keep your eyes from getting lost in all the shadow, define your top and bottom lashlines with a soft-black liner pencil."

" Don't have white shadow? Create starry details on your eyes with a white pencil instead."

" Pairing the dark shadow with a pop of color at your brow keeps the look from being too goth."

YOUR EDGY LOOK BOOK

ZAC POSEN

With eyes this bright, stick with nude lip gloss and skip the blush.

ANNA SUI

Toss the rules out the window and trace eyeliner above— *way* above—your top lashline.

EMMA WATSON

Gold metallic touches on the inner *and* outer "v" of your eyes give a smoky look without washing you out.

KRISTEN STEWART

Get smoldering eyes with a wash of gray. The look is intense, but in a soft way!

DSQUARED2

You'll leave everyone else starry-eyed when you mix gold and silver loose glitter!

V V BROWN

A winged eye is classic—but adding a frosty white shadow up to the browbone takes it to a whole new level.

Get inspired by these celeb and runway looks— the makeup possibilities are endless!

3.1 PHILLIP LIM

A fresh new way to wear metallic: Apply it on inner eye corners and create a crescent shape into crease.

KENDALL JENNER

For a bold look that won't budge on the dance floor, use a waterproof liner and mascara.

JESSIE J

You have the confidence to wear a daring hot-pink lipstick. Swipe it on and work it!

DONNA KARAN

Dominate your hallway with bold brows *and* lips. Keep the rest of the face clean and natural.

MIRANDA COSGROVE

Sometimes a touch of edge is all you need: Line lower lashlines with a smoky brown for subtle drama.

ROONEY MARA

Take a walk on the bright side with vivid shadow! Just stick with neutral lips and a teensy bit of blush.

SHIMMERY BRONZER

The golden flecks give you **a radiant glow** for a finish that's pure (and glowy!) perfection.

TINTED MOISTURIZER WITH SPF

Even out your complexion with an **easy swipe of color** *and* protect your skin from the sun.

CORAL LIPSTICK

Golden undertones **add luster and interest** to a simple coral lip color.

AQUA CREAM SHADOW

Smudge along your top lid for a **tropical gleam**!

BLUSH PEBBLES

Warm up your cheeks with **soft mineral blush.**

boho

The boho look is earthy and natural but goes way beyond blah neutrals. Pair your everyday fresh face with washes of nature-inspired color— peacock blues, leafy greens, or warm sunset shades. Don't worry about the rules—the best looks always come together organically.

MARBLEIZED SHADOW STICK

A swirl of soft shades in a single, **easy-to-use shadow stick**—boho heaven!

SHEER PEACHY GLOSS

It adds just the right amount of **pretty brightness** to your kiss!

ULTIMATE *boho* LOOKS

These four free-spirited looks will take you anywhere!

STEP 1:
For a **healthy-looking glow,** mix a few drops of liquid bronzer into your moisturizer, then apply it all over your face. It'll warm up your complexion and give you a hint of sparkle.

17 TIP:
Bold eyes look best with a simple face! Stick with cheek and lip shades that are close to your natural skin tone—you'll look pretty in a super-chill way.

STEP 3:
A nude gloss **polishes the look.** To prevent goopiness, blot your lips on the back of your hand (a tissue will make them sticky!).

STEP 2:
Forest-colored shadows add drama to a neutral face! Use a more vivid green along the lashline and crease, and a pop of gold on the center of your lid for a pretty application that's just right for school.

school

Emerald eyes paired with a golden shimmer are a fresh mix for class.

STEP 1:

Give relaxed makeup a **radiant hit**! Blend shimmery highlighter above your cheekbones and just below your brows.

STEP 2:

For a fast, pulled-together look, sweep **golden-peach cheek color** onto your apples.

STEP 3:

For **mellow color** that'll last through an entire afternoon, fill in your lips completely with a nude lip pencil, then add a coat of lip balm!

STEP 4:

Graze the mascara wand over just the ends of your lashes to bring out your eyes in a **subtle way.**

weekend

Soft coral shades pack a peachy punch—but they're casual enough for a breezy day hanging out with friends.

date

Neutral metallics look dressy but not overdone— just right for a lunch date or flirty movie.

STEP 1:
Draw attention to your eyes with a stroke of **glittery** shadow on your lids.

STEP 2:
Add **instant warmth** without cakiness with an allover dusting of lightweight loose powder blush.

STEP 3:
A swipe of a gold lipstick with a rosy tinge won't wash you out and makes your complexion look **luminous.**

party

Experiment with pool-inspired color combos. They'll give your face a splash of fun!

17 TIP:
Smudge! Use your fingers to soften and blend your blush and shadow—hard edges can make bright colors look stamped on.

STEP 1:

Look **flawless** all day with a sheer foundation. The result is a little dewy, a little polished.

STEP 2:

Bright, exotic shades of shadow and liner create a sexy nighttime look. Try a sweep of eyeliner on your top lashline, or kick it up a notch by smudging matching shadow all around your eyes.

STEP 3:

A **sheer, tropical lip color** is a fun alternative to matte lipstick—it won't compete with your eyes.

TOP *boho* SECRETS

Try these tricks from Hollywood's top makeup artists!

Kylie Jenner

1 ADD A WASH OF COLOR!

"For a really natural flush, apply moisturizer followed by a liquid stain on your cheeks. You can almost see through it—like you're actually blushing."
–Mario Dedivanovic

2 TRY AN EARTHY EYESHADOW!

"Rust-colored shadow is unexpectedly flattering but still neutral. It looks so gorgeous in the crease of a brown-eyed girl or on the lower lid of a blue-eyed girl." **–Autumn Moultrie**

Dakota Fanning

3 FAKE SUN-KISSED SKIN!

"Dust bronzer where the sun would naturally warm up your skin—over your forehead, along the cheekbones, onto your chin, and even on your nose!" –**Mylah Morales**

Zoë Kravitz

Whitney Port

4 GO FOR LOW-KEY LIPS!

"Hate obvious-looking lip color? I use tinted balm! It'll make your lip color a little more vivid without hard, makeup-y edges."
–**Brett Freedman**

Shay Mitchell

5 LIGHTEN UP YOUR LASHES!

"Brown is a great alternative to black—it looks more natural. Or, if your lashes are naturally long and dark, curl them and just use a clear formula for glossiness."
–**Coleen Campbell-Olwell**

Christie

AGE: 17

HOMETOWN: Long Island, NY

STAR SIGN: Virgo

FAVE COLOR: Mint green

HOBBIES: Jazz and lyrical dance
(a blend of ballet and modern),
playing the violin, science

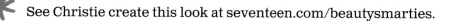

I wear bright makeup colors for my dance performances, but offstage my everyday makeup is a lot more understated and simple.

✳ See Christie create this look at seventeen.com/beautysmarties.

MY FAVORITE PLACE

"I can't get enough of **the beach.** I even go there during the fall and winter to walk around. I love the crisp air."

MY MUST-HAVE

"I like **eco-friendly beauty products** that are natural and pretty."

MY FAVORITE TRICK

"I use **gold shimmer powder** on the inner corners of my eyes. It makes them look so much brighter."

my inspirations

MY FASHION OBSESSION

"I'm into **statement jewelry,** like bib necklaces and large cuffs. They give my laid-back outfits a bit of edge."

MY BEAUTY OBSESSION

"**Glimmery pressed eyeshadows.** They're a really nice texture, and they stay on forever. They're great for my dance competitions."

MY CELEB CRUSH

"**Blake Lively.** She always has great, natural-looking makeup."

BEST TRICK

"A **sheer, dark lip gloss** is a good way to ease yourself into wearing more intense colors."

Christie's look:
NATURAL SHIMMER

"I love looking like I just threw something on, and this makeup gives that effect. I'd wear it anywhere."

SHADE
" Use a coppery metallic shadow stick to shade your lid from lash to brow. The **golden tones** make it warmer and more wearable."

LINE
" Trace the shadow stick on the **outer corners of your lower lashline,** too. It adds extra pop and makes the smoky eyes look put together."

" Sheer blush lets your skin show through for natural-looking rosiness. No need to set with powder— your skin will look glowier without it."

SWIPE
" Get a **luminous glow** by applying a light coral tone to your cheekbones. With a brush, swirl the blush onto the apples of your cheeks, blending lightly upward."

SHINE
" **Pinky nude gloss** is soft and pretty, and fits the natural vibe of this makeup."

" My eyes stand out more when I fill in my brows with a brown pencil or powder. To blend it, I run a brush through the hairs."

77

YOUR *boho* LOOK BOOK

DSQUARED2

A quick way to get luminous skin: Dust your face with a sheer mineral foundation.

ZOË KRAVITZ

Punch up earth tones with deeper terra-cotta shades on eyes and lips.

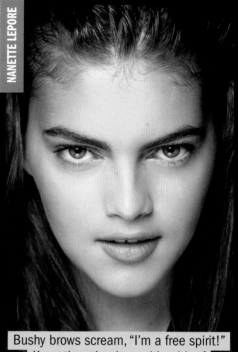

NANETTE LEPORE

Bushy brows scream, "I'm a free spirit!" Keep them in place with a bit of hair gel and an old, clean toothbrush.

PAUL & JOE

Accent your fave features with touches of platinum shimmer on inner eye corners and center of lips.

VICTORIA JUSTICE

Tap on lipstick with your finger to get a subtle stain—it'll look like you were eating berries!

MARY-KATE OLSEN

Do smoky eyes the boho way—line your inner lids, then use an earthy shadow shade like copper all around your eyes.

Get inspired by these celeb and runway looks— the makeup possibilities are endless!

CHLOÉ

Mocha eyeshadow really pops when paired with thick, defined lashes.

LEA MICHELE

Got killer cheekbones? Flaunt them by dusting bronze powder in the hollows of your cheeks and out toward your temples.

J. MENDEL

Create easy nude lips by dabbing concealer over your pout, then adding a clear gloss or lip balm on top.

ASHLEY GREENE

Coral on cheeks and lips wakes up your whole face—and the color looks amazing on *all* skin tones!

NAYA RIVERA

Lush lashes make your eyes flirty and bright: Apply two coats of lengthening mascara on top and bottom lashes.

JASON WU

Let the bright colors of autumn inspire your look! Leafy metallic eyes hit the right note.

YOUR ULTIMATE hair guide

MOUSSE

Scrunch it onto damp hair to coax out your **natural hair texture**!

DOUBLE-BARRELED CURLING IRON

Gives you **natural looking waves** in just one clamp!

HEADBAND

Dresses up your texture instantly!

VELCRO ROLLERS

Use them all over to create **luscious, glamorous waves**!

DIFFUSER

Releases **a gentle flow of air** to dry your strands quickly without disturbing your natural wave or curl pattern.

CURL-DEFINING CREAM

Just a dollop adds **pretty definition** to your hair.

waves & curls

The beauty of waves and curls is that they can look as unique as the girl who rocks them. Wear them soft and loose for an ultra-feminine feel, or tousle and tease them to unleash your inner wild child!

DUCKBILL CLIPS

Slide them in while drying your hair to **lift up your roots** so they don't fall flat against your scalp.

ULTIMATE *waves*

These four lush looks will take you anywhere!

STEP 1:
Spritz on a **heat-protector spray** and wrap sections of hair around **large hot rollers.** Leave them in for 15 minutes.

STEP 2:
Undo the rollers and **brush through the waves** to loosen them up. Then **tease the ends** for a tousled effect.

STEP 3:
Pull back one side of your hair with a pretty pin and **do a little more teasing** in the front. Finish with hairspray for long-lasting hold.

date

Soft, touchable waves strike the perfect balance between sexy and approachable.

& curls

17 TIP: Hydrate! Naturally curly hair tends to be dry, so be sure to deep condition weekly for bouncy, happy strands.

STEP 1:
Flip your head upside down and **fluff your curls** with your fingers to boost body.

STEP 2:
Lightly mist hair with a **curl-enhancing spray** to de-frizz and add a little definition.

STEP 3:
For volume in the front, make a side part, then loosely grab one side of your hair and pin it back. Pull back the other side and push it forward toward your hairline to **create a casual pouf.** Secure with pins and go!

weekend

A chic bump adds structure to messy, slept-on curls (and no one will know it took only two minutes)!

STEP 1:

Create lots of volume with a dollop of **moisturizing mousse**! Apply it to your hair while it's still damp.

STEP 2:

Use a **diffuser** to bring out tons of texture as you dry. Lift and scrunch your strands as you go.

STEP 3:

For deliberate messiness, tease your hair all over with a **boar-bristle brush.** Start at the ends and work your way up.

STEP 4:

A stack of bobby pins on one side **adds a little sweetness** to your look.

party

Change up your going-out look! Try one that's wild and untamed— you'll have a ball turning heads!

STEP 1:
Spray towel-dried hair with curl-defining mousse for **hold and volume.**

STEP 2:
Twirl your hair around your fingers as you **dry it with a diffuser** to help keep the shape.

STEP 3:
To **sculpt ropy ringlets,** hold your curling iron vertically and wind sections of hair around the barrel. Release after ten seconds.

STEP 4:
When you're done curling, lightly finger-comb hair, then **clip back the front** for a relaxed effect.

school

Easy, non-uniform curls look good even if they start to fall—perfect for a long day of classes.

TOP *waves &*

Try these tricks from Hollywood's top stylists!

1 DEFINE YOUR WAVES!

"Apply a shine serum to random pieces of hair. It will give a messy style some dimension so it still looks polished."
—Ken Paves

Aly Michalka

2 SLEEP ON IT!

" For truly natural-looking texture, braid small sections of damp hair and pin them up. Air-dry, then shake out your hair." —Campbell McAuley

Emma Stone

curls SECRETS

3 ROCK YOUR ROLLERS!

"Use your rollers to create different looks. If you want big, bouncy hair, roll the hair starting at the ends all the way to the roots. If you want waves, place the roller at the scalp and roll the hair around the roller, wrapping from roots to ends."
–Mark Townsend

Miranda Cosgrove

5 ADD SOME FRILL!

"Frilly hair accessories give your waves a special girly touch. It's an easy and cheap way to update your style!"
–Charles Baker Strahan

4 LOOK NATURALLY TOUSLED!

"For that just-got-up texture, mix a drop of oil with smoothing cream in your hands and rake the product into your dry hair from mid-length down. Rub your fingers to the ends for naturally defined strands." **–Mark Townsend**

Nikki Reed

Rihanna

Ashley

AGE: 16

HOMETOWN: Edmonton, Alberta, Canada

STAR SIGN: Cancer

FAVE COLORS: White, silver, and purple

HOBBIES: Shopping, horseback riding, going to the beach

> **I curl my hair basically every time I style it—I'll do anything from big, retro curls to tight spirals.**

✳ See Ashley create this look at seventeen.com/beautysmarties.

MY BEAUTY OBSESSION

" **Intense-hold volumizing** hairspray! I've been using it for years. It makes my curls last all day and also adds amazing volume!"

MY BEAUTY ICON

" **Marilyn Monroe**. Her hair was always so fabulous, and so was she."

MY STYLING STAPLE

" A **wide-tooth comb.** I always comb through my hair when it's wet to get rid of tangles."

MY CELEB CRUSH

" I love the way **Selena Gomez**'s curls have so much volume—her hair looks phenomenal."

my inspirations

MY FASHION MUST-HAVE

" I love **leather** pants, dresses, jackets and tops. Leather makes waves look even sexier!"

MY ESSENTIAL TOOL

" I love my **curling iron.** It can create tight, structured curls or loose flowy waves. No matter what I go for, it comes out looking glamorous."

Ashley's look:
THE BIG BOUNCE

"I love the fact that this look can be done in a short amount of time but it looks so put together!"

HOW-TO:

CURL

"**A large curling iron** creates big, loose waves. Wind your hair around the iron, but leave out the ends for a casual, almost beachy effect."

TWIST

"**Pull the front pieces back** to add a unique twist. Take small sections on each side and twist them all the way down to the ends."

SECURE

"**Bring the twists together** at the back of your head and keep them perfectly in place with pins. Brush through the ends to blend them into the rest of your hair."

"Volumizing hairspray makes my curls last all day and also adds amazing body!"

"I use a heat-protector serum to keep my hair from getting fried from my daily curling sessions."

"A ceramic curling iron helps protect my hair from heat damage."

YOUR *waves & curls*

SELENA GOMEZ

Go flirty with big, loose waves. Make big coils with a large barrel curling iron then brush through to smooth them out.

ANNALYNNE McCORD

Be sure to give natural curls the moisture they crave. Apply a leave-in conditioner to damp hair and air-dry.

KEKE PALMER

Ombré hair color gradually gets lighter toward the ends—it adds pretty dimension to curly styles.

BELLA THORNE

Make a curly style quirky by pinning a whimsical flower (or two!) on one side.

KATY PERRY

Clip in a few different colored extensions around your face for pops of brightness!

BETSEY JOHNSON

Add extra glamour to your look with a deep side part and by sweeping curls to one side.

LOOK BOOK

Get inspired by these celeb and runway looks—the possibilities are endless!

REBECCA MINKOFF

Channel a hippie chick with fluffy, undone waves. Brush through dry ringlets with a paddle brush, then tease with a rattail comb.

ZENDAYA

For boing-y curls that last, roll up sections with your fingers and pin them to your head. Blow-dry, undo the pins, then clip your curls over one shoulder.

RAG & BONE

Tousle natural waves with your fingers as you blow-dry for perfectly imperfect texture.

JORDIN SPARKS

To keep natural curls perfectly defined, comb them only when they're wet.

CAMILLA BELLE

Smooth some hair over your forehead and tuck it behind your ear for a dose of sophistication.

MILEY CYRUS

For ultracool matte texture, sprinkle dry shampoo over your waves and massage it in.

METAL CUFFED BANDS

Wrap one around the base of a braid for a **cool alternative** to a basic black band.

POMADE

Before you start braiding, **rough up your texture** with this. It keeps your braid looking undone.

TEXTURIZING SPRAY

Creates a **cool, matte finish** for the ultimate beachy feel!

MEGA-HOLD GEL

Keeps your style in place **all day**!

MINI ELASTICS

The smaller size gives the end of your braid **a neater look.**

braids & twists

They're just the thing when you want to liven up your hair—and so easy, you could make a simple one with your eyes closed. But when you want to get noticed, go beyond the braid basics— all it takes is a little bit of imagination to create an unforgettable look.

SMALL CURLING IRON

Perfect for **curling** the pieces that fall around your face.

ULTIMATE *braids & twists*

These four creative looks will take you anywhere!

STEP 1:

Give your hair a sleek base by dabbing a little gel onto the sides of your hair then brushing them down. **Make low pigtails,** leaving out a chunk of hair on each side.

STEP 2:

Wrap the loose pieces of hair around the elastics at the base of your ponies and pin. **Split each pigtail in half** and twist the two sections around each other. **Wrap an elastic** a thumb's width from the ends.

STEP 3:

Pin the ends to the base of the pigtail to make big loops. **Finish with shine spray.**

weekend

Weekends were made for a minimal-effort style, like these playful twisted twin loops.

17 TIP:
Separate your hair into equal sections so your braids look neat—not lopsided.

STEP 1:
For edgy, slept-in texture, **spritz hair with a beach spray.** Make a side part with your fingers, then air-dry or use a diffuser.

STEP 2:
Create a side part, then **loosely gather your hair** so it swoops down your forehead. Use a bobby pin to hold it in place behind your ear.

STEP 3:
Grab a couple of sections from behind your ears and braid them tightly. Use **small, clear elastics** at the ends for a clean finish.

school

Fast mini braids are perfect for days when your schedule is jam-packed!

STEP 1:

For shine and hold, create a side part and **apply pomade** to dry hair.

STEP 2:

Take a wide section of hair and start making a **Dutch braid** on the side opposite your part. Braid your hair and add in pieces from each side, pulling the pieces *underneath* the braid as you go.

STEP 3:

When you get to your ear, stop braiding and pull the rest of your hair into a **low side ponytail.** Twist it into a **bun** and secure with bobby pins and hairspray.

date

This pretty braided bun is special enough to give you tons of confidence but so easy to do.

STEP 1:

For better grip when braiding, **sprinkle dry shampoo** all over your hair, then create a side part.

STEP 2:

Braid hair into a **fishtail:** Split your hair into two even sections. Pull a skinny strand of hair from the outside of the left section and add to the right side. Repeat on the right side. Keep going until you get to the ends, then secure with a **cute accessory.**

STEP 3:

Gently **tug strands** from the sides of the braid to create those cool, carefree wisps. A dab of wax will give the braid definition.

party

The messier this style gets, the cooler it looks—you'll have a blast all night without any hair stress!

TOP *braids & twists* SECRETS

Try these tricks from Hollywood's top stylists!

Vanessa Hudgens

1 RECYCLE YOUR BRAID!

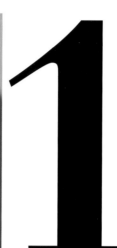

"The day after you wear a braid, you can use the texture to create a new look. Leave the braid in overnight, then in the morning, undo the braid and flip your head upside down and shake it out. Brush your hair, add a little bit of styling cream, then make a loose bun. The kinky effect from the braid looks natural and cool."
–Christian Marc

2 USE "INVISIBLE" ELASTICS!

"Use the small, clear elastics for braids. That way, the elastic disappears into the finished look and the attention stays focused on the braid or the twist."
–Aaron Light

Elizabeth Olsen

3

TAME LITTLE HAIRS!

"Smooth a lightweight styling cream through the hair before weaving it together to get rid of flyaways. It's okay if there are a few little imperfections still left in the hair—they make the look more interesting."
–**Charles Baker Strahan**

Dianna Agron

Bella Thorne

4

SWITCH UP YOUR FISHTAIL!

"Fishtail braids can be a little tricky for beginners to do. To make it easier, braid your hair while it's wet—it's easier to control." –**Rod Ortega**

Nina Dobrev

5

GET CREATIVE!

"There are so many things you can use to secure a braid besides an elastic. Try a ribbon, raffia, or, if you want a seamless look, you could even tie the end of your braid with sewing thread." –**Rod Ortega**

103

seventeen
BEAUTY
SMARTIES

Laura

AGE: 17

HOMETOWN: Cumberland, ME

STAR SIGN: Libra

FAVE COLOR: Pink

HOBBIES: Playing with makeup, spending time with family and friends, shopping

My style is very simple. I don't like to be over-the-top, but I like to look put together.

 See Laura create this look at seventeen.com/beautysmarties.

MY CELEB CRUSH

"**Lauren Conrad.** She has amazing style in general, but she is known for her **braided hairstyles.** They are so unique, yet they are simple to re-create."

MY SURPRISE ACCESSORY

"A **red rose** is so elegant and beautiful—and it looks great tucked into a braided updo."

MY PRODUCT OBSESSION

"Serum. I use it when my hair is damp after I shower. It adds **shine and smoothness,** eliminates frizz, and smells amazing."

my inspirations

TREND I LOVE

"**Fishtail braids.** They look so unique and complicated, but they can be as easy as a regular braid with a little practice!"

MY FAVORITE PLACE

"I love being around nature. When I see a **beautiful landscape,** a sunset, or an ocean, I am instantly happy."

MY FAVORITE ACCESSORY

"**Scarves.** They don't need to be expensive to be beautiful. I use small ones on the end of my braids to dress them up."

Laura's look:
COOL CROWN

"This braid looks very intricate but is actually easy to create!"

"Hairspray will keep your braid smooth and together."

HOW-TO:

SMOOTH

"**Blow-dry** your hair first so it's nice and sleek—that makes it easier to braid. Then make a **deep side part** and start an inside-out braid on the other side of it. To do it, you cross the hair under rather than over."

BRAID

"Keep **braiding slowly and neatly around your head** until you get to just below your other ear. If you're a beginning braider, you can always have a friend do this for you—it's tricky when you can't see the back!"

WRAP

"**Tie the end of the braid** with an elastic, and cover it with a small piece of your hair. Leave the rest hanging down for a cool ponytail-braid hybrid."

"Apply a smoothing cream and make sure that your hair is completely brushed out before starting. That makes it easier to create the braid without any bumps or tangles."

"For extra sleekness, run a flat-iron over the tail."

YOUR *braids & twists*

ARIEL WINTER

Sophisticated curls look more fun when you add a few cute twists in the front.

SARAH HYLAND

For a casual braided ponytail, braid your hair halfway and leave the ends loose.

CARLOS MIELE

Combine a pony and a braid: Wear it high on the head to give this girly look a more modern edge.

WHITNEY PORT

To give a braided updo a dose of edginess, let pieces of hair fall down around your face.

ANGELA SIMMONS

A quick way to keep your hair back: Roll a small section in the front back toward your crown and secure with a bobby pin.

HAILEE STEINFELD

When a girly mood strikes you, try this sweet style. Secure your side braid with a sparkly bow barrette, leaving out an inch or two at the end.

LOOK BOOK

Get inspired by these celeb and runway looks—the possibilities are endless!

AMBER HEARD

Create loads of interest with multiple braids! Loop them together into a bun in the back for a look that lasts.

RIHANNA

For hair down to there, add clip-in extensions, then make your braid extralong.

KENZO

When you add pompadour bangs, even pigtails can look totally rock and roll!

JENNIFER HUDSON

Make a side braid special-occasion-worthy by swooping hair down into a loop pinned above your ear, then braiding the hair beneath it.

ELLE FANNING

For milkmaid braids, braid two pigtails, then pin them across the top of your head.

BLAKE LIVELY

Cap off a sideswept, messy style with tiny braids. They peek through the strands for a pretty, unexpected surprise!

CLARIFYING SHAMPOO/ CONDITIONER

Washes away buildup from styling products so hair is more manageable.

HEAT PROTECTANT

Safeguards your strands from *all* hot tools.

HEADBAND

Easily **transitions** your look from school to party!

HAIR TOWEL

The super-absorbent material is made to soak up water quickly for **faster blow-drying**!

MINI IRON

Smooth your bangs (or a short cut) in one effortless sweep!

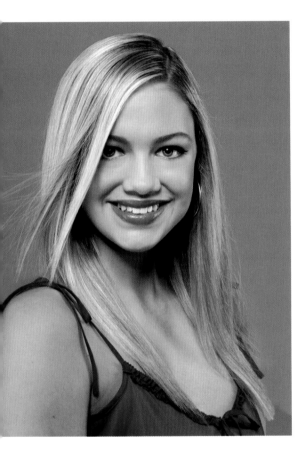

sleek

Super-straight hair is undeniably sophisticated. But a subtle change in detail can instantly update the vibe: Blunt ends add a dose of edge, a slight curve on the bottom gives a pretty feel, and a sparkly accessory ups the glam level.

WIDE-TOOTH COMB

Leaves even the most tangled hair smooth and **knot-free** in seconds.

HAIR VITAMINS/ SUPPLEMENTS

Strengthens your hair against breakage and split ends.

ULTIMATE *sleek* LOOKS

These four polished looks will take you anywhere!

STEP 1:
Use the tip of a fine-tooth comb to separate out your bangs (or long layers in the front) and to **create a defined part** in front of your crown. Spritz a root-lifter onto damp hair, then blow-dry.

STEP 2:
Tease the crown with the comb for volume, then smooth out the top layer.

STEP 3:
For soft, romantic texture, **curl the ends** of your hair around a large boar-bristle brush, **blast with a blow-dryer** for 30 seconds, then unravel. To add gloss, finish with a spritz of shine spray.

17 TIP:
For long or really fine hair that needs volume, bend over and blow-dry your hair upside down.

date

Go all-out sexy with a touch of volume, peekaboo bangs, and a barely there bend at the ends.

STEP 1:

Gather your bangs across your forehead and **finger-comb** them into place—hair is easier to style if you style it just how you want it **before** you use a flat-iron.

STEP 2:

For longer-lasting sleekness, apply a **smoothing balm** to your dry strands—it helps fight humidity and annoying frizz.

STEP 3:

Working in small sections, slowly glide a **flat-iron** down the entire length of your hair. When you're done, apply **styling wax** to your ends for cool, piecey texture.

school

Soft-swept bangs and glossy layers frame your face for a low-key, ultra-flattering look.

STEP 1:

To fake major length, add a **super-long clip-in extension** piece. Part your hair horizontally above your ears, and clip the top half of your hair out of the way. Snap the faux piece onto the bottom section of hair. Let your natural hair down and finger-comb it all together to blend.

STEP 2:

Tease the front section of your hair with a fine-tooth comb, then use the comb to smooth a thin layer of hair on top over the bump to hide the messiness.

STEP 3:

Dab some gel onto the sides of your hair, brush them back, and secure them under the front section with bobby pins that match your hair color. **Spritz hairspray all over** for partyproof hold.

party

Take the typical sleek half-updo to the next level with a futuristic double side part.

STEP 1:

Make a deep side part, then **flat-iron your hair from roots** to tips (spritz each section with a heat protector before you straighten it).

STEP 2:

Brush the wide front section of hair over one side of your forehead and behind your ears. **Make a low ponytail,** leaving out a small piece of hair underneath the base.

STEP 3:

Wrap the extra section of hair around the elastic and secure. To keep your ends smooth, **slick on some antifrizz cream.**

weekend

Slick, sideswept bangs give a simple pony just enough polish for carefree days.

TOP *sleek* SECRETS

Try these tricks from Hollywood's top stylists.

1 SPLURGE ON TOOLS!

" Investing in high-quality tools will save you money in the long run. You'll need fewer styling products and trips to the salon because your hair will be in better shape. And a good flat-iron can last years!"
–Rod Ortega

Jessica Szohr

2 TRY FAUX FRINGE!

" To switch up a straight style, clip-in bangs are a great option. To attach them, separate the front center section of your hair, then tie it back. Clip in the fake bangs over the sectioned hair several finger-widths from your hairline, then use your fingers or a comb to blend them in with your real hair." **–Ursula Stephen**

Lauren Conrad

Zendaya

3 PLAY WITH YOUR PART!

"To get a more professional sleek look—like for going to an interview—go with a side part. It looks more polished than a center part, which tends to look more romantic or glamorous."-**Ron Ortega**

Elle Fanning

4 BOOST BODY!

"To create more volume, do your blowout with a round brush and lift up the roots as you do each section. You'll give your whole style more movement so it doesn't fall flat." –**Christian Marc**

Kristen Stewart

5 ZAP GREASY ROOTS!

"Don't let a straight style look lifeless! Sprinkle or spray dry shampoo onto the roots of your hair to suck up oil. It gives you instant volume." –**Christian Marc**

Arden

AGE: 16

HOMETOWN: Little Rock, AR

STAR SIGN: Taurus

FAVE COLOR: Red

HOBBIES: Cheerleading, watching *30 Rock*, making YouTube videos

> **Straight hair is simple but cool, which is a great match for effortless style. It works with jeans and a white T-shirt *or* a little black dress.**

 See Arden create this look at seventeen.com/beautysmarties.

MY BEAUTY ICON

"**Audrey Hepburn.** She's an example of how to be poised and classy but still have fun!"

MY ESSENTIAL TOOL

"My **ceramic flat-iron** gives me amazingly straight hair."

MY MUST-HAVE

"I love **cute, trendy hair accessories** that don't cost a lot."

MY FASHION OBSESSION

"**Oversize sweaters!** Anything that makes me look like I actually have a boyfriend that I can steal clothes from is worth wearing! Plus, I like the contrast between a casual sweater and smooth, shiny hair."

my inspirations

JAMIE CHUNG

MY CELEB CRUSH

"I really admire **Mila Kunis.** Her hair always looks so smooth and touchable."

MY SECRET WEAPON

"**Silicone-based blow-dry lotion.** It makes your hair silky and super-touchable. My hairdresser once used it on me when he was styling my hair for my winter formal. I fell in love!"

Arden's look:
SWEPT AWAY

"If you use blow-dry lotion, apply it sparingly—a quarter-size dab will do. You want to look sleek, not greasy!"

"This style is truly universal—it's a go-anywhere, do-anything kind of look."

PART

" Create a defined side part, then **blow-dry the front** with a round brush, placing brush over (rather than under) hair to create a sideswept effect. Blow-dry the rest of your hair at a downward angle."

PREP

"To get a perfectly smooth texture, **go over your blow-dried hair with a flat-iron,** paying extra attention to any stubborn waves."

POLISH

"Use a bit of **shine serum on the bottom half of your hair** or your ends to make them look glossy and even sleeker."

" I like to brush through my hair a few times after I'm done with the flat-iron to make it look really silky and soft."

"Mini flat-irons are great for bangs or shorter hair—it's easier to get to the roots."

121

YOUR *sleek* LOOK BOOK

NANETTE LEPORE

A few long, choppy layers in front help fine, straight hair look fuller.

WHITNEY PORT

For this much glossiness, apply a shine serum to damp hair before you do a blowout. Add a smidge more to your ends when you're done.

JESSIE J

Blow-dry blunt, brow-grazing bangs with a paddle brush—a round brush can leave bangs looking too curved.

VANESSA HUDGENS

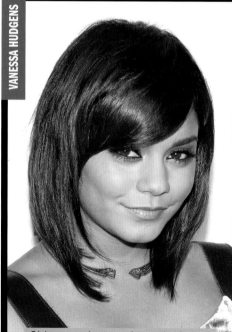

Sideswept bangs always look sexy with a midlength cut. Or, if you have long layers in the front, just tuck them behind your ear.

EMMA STONE

Keep layers around your face looking sharp and defined by flat-ironing just the ends.

DEREK LAM

For a modern vibe, neatly pin back the front section.

Get inspired by these celeb and runway looks—
the possibilities are endless!

LUCY HALE

Give French-girl chicness to straight hair by topping it with a floppy black beret.

JASON WU

A smoothing cream tames every single hair so you can pull it back tightly without a flyaway!

KEKE PALMER

If your hair is relaxed, try blowing it out with a comb attachment on your blow-dryer instead of a brush—it's gentler on fragile strands.

L.A.M.B.

Use a midsize curling iron to add a little body to the ends of a short, straight style.

SHAILENE WOODLEY

Look effortlessly chic with a loose, half-up style. Pin the sides ever-so-slightly back with a bobby pin and let them fall naturally.

EMMA WATSON

Mix a little gel with styling cream for hair that looks slick but not too stiff.

NO-SLIP PONYTAIL HOLDERS

They glide onto your hair with ease and **stay put.**

REPAIR SERUM

Keeps your strands **healthy and strong** so they don't break from being pulled tight.

SMALL FLAT-IRON

It gets the frizzies along your hairline **under control** fast!

HAIR EXTENSIONS

Fake a fuller, longer look instantly with **easy-to-use** clip-ons.

COLORFUL PINS

Add a little fun to your look and **hold loose wisps** in place.

ponies

Ponytails are the beauty equivalent to jeans: They're so versatile, easy, and chic, you could practically live in them! Luckily, there's a version for any occasion—and they look as good at the gym as they can at prom.

SMOOTHING HAIR CREAM

When you want soft hold and a **super-glossy look.**

MIXED-BRISTLE BRUSH

It helps to **smooth** down every single flyaway.

ULTIMATE ponies

These four go-to looks will take you anywhere!

STEP 1:
For major glossiness, rub a dime-size amount of **shine serum** through your hair (but skip the roots so they don't get greasy!).

STEP 2:
Brush your hair up into a **tight ponytail** and secure with an elastic.

STEP 3:
To give the ends some bounce, wrap the bottom few inches of the tail around a **large-barrel curling iron**.

school

For those "Why didn't my alarm go off?!" mornings, an ultra-sleek pony is the chicest I-meant-to-do-this answer.

STEP 1:

For pretty sleekness, apply a **straightening balm** to damp hair, then **blow-dry.** Go over the bottom half of your hair with a **flat-iron** for extra polish.

STEP 2:

Brush hair back into a **snug, high pony.** Smooth any lumps with a **fine-tooth comb.**

STEP 3:

For a Grecian effect, tie a **gold cord** around the base of your pony, leaving two long pieces on either side. Crisscross them along your tail. Wrap them tightly around the ends a few times, knot the cord, then snip off the rest.

party

A simple style with one striking, unexpected detail is the ultimate conversation starter.

STEP 1:

For soft texture, make **big coils** all over your head with a **large-barrel curling** iron, then brush through them to make soft waves.

STEP 2:

Split your hair down the middle into **two sections.** Braid each piece behind your ear, leaving out a small section underneath each side. Stop braiding about a third of the way down, then **secure with an elastic.**

STEP 3:

Wrap the loose pieces of hair around the bands and secure with bobby pins for a pretty, put-together look. Finish with a mist of **light-hold hairspray.**

date

Double your flirt factor with sweet pigtails!
Piecey twists give the look a bit of edge.

17 TIP:
If you've got super-thick hair, use barrettes instead of elastics. An elastic might only make it around your pony once or twice, but a barrette will lock it into place.

STEP 1:
Keep frizz in check with a dab of **moisturizing styling cream** on dry hair.

STEP 2:
Create a side part, then pull a small section of hair in the front into a side ponytail using a **colored rubber band.**

STEP 3:
Tie all of your hair together at the nape of your neck with another **bold band.** Add one more elastic a few inches down.

STEP 4:
Using a **vented brush,** gently loosen the hair between the bands for a fun "bubble" effect.

weekend

Swap out basic black bands for punchy colored elastics to add a bright pop to your pony.

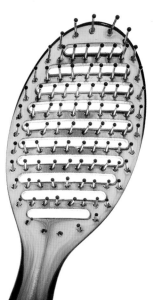

TOP pony SECRETS

Try these tricks from Hollywood's top stylists!

1 DRESS UP YOUR DO!

"I love to dress up a ponytail with something special—like a crystal headband or a wide piece of colored satin from the fabric store."
–Mark Townsend

Julianne Hough

Nina Dobrev

2 BUMP IT UP!

"Transform an everyday ponytail into a flirty style by adding a bump to the top! Split hair in half horizontally and secure the bottom with an elastic. Back-comb the top for volume and combine the two halves into one ponytail." **–Allan Avendano**

3

TRY SOMETHING FUN!

"Colorful clip-in extensions add a bit of edge to a ponytail—and they're not permanent, so it's easy to do it for just one night." –Ursula Stephen

Kat Graham

AnnaLynne McCord

4

ADD BOUNCE!

"For nice bounce, separate your tail into a few sections, curl each one with a large-barrel curling iron, then brush and tease them a little bit. This looks great with a ponytail that's positioned in the center of your head—it makes a beautiful profile."
–Christian Marc

Miley Cyrus

5

AVOID HAIR BREAKAGE!

"Make sure to use snag-free ponytail elastics—stay away from ponytail holders that have metal clamps!" –Mark Townsend

seventeen
BEAUTY
SMARTIES

Bethany

AGE: 16

HOMETOWN: Los Banos, CA

STAR SIGN: Scorpio

FAVE COLOR: Pink

HOBBIES: Shopping,
helping girls look their best,
making videos

"I like to keep my hair simple, but I always add some curls or waves. A little bit of texture makes it look more dolled up."

See Bethany create this look at seventeen.com/beautysmarties.

MY BEST STYLING TRICK

"My best friend taught me to take a small piece of hair from my ponytail and wrap it around the elastic—it looks so much more **polished**."

MY FINISHING TOUCH

"I always want my hair to smell as good as it looks. So after it's done, I like to spray it with a little **perfume.** When I hug people, they always tell me I smell great!"

MY LITTLE HAIR HELPER

"A **teasing comb** for volume!"

my inspirations

MY FASHION OBSESSION

"I wear **riding boots** all the time. They're a casual yet chic look—perfect with ponytails."

MY MAGIC COMBO

"I mix **leave-in conditioner with hair oil.** It keeps my hair looking healthy and feeling soft."

MY CELEB CRUSH

"**Jessica Alba** always has the most stunning and unique ponytails on the red carpet!"

Bethany's look:
SWEET SWING

"I wear ponytails like this all the time when I go out. Teasing at the roots and wrapping the base makes it more dressy."

HOW-TO:

BLOW OUT

"To create a **smooth foundation** for the style, blow-dry your hair with a big round brush. Add a **nozzle attachment** to the dryer to concentrate the air exactly where you want it. You'll get sleeker results."

CURL

"**Pull all of your hair up** into a ponytail except for a piece wide enough to wrap around the pony. **Curl your tail** in small sections by wrapping each piece around a clipless curling iron."

COVER

"Break apart the curls with your fingers so they don't look too defined. Then **wrap the loose piece of hair** around the base of the pony and secure with pins for a girlier, more finished look."

"Use a strong-hold hairspray on the curls to make sure they maintain their shape."

"Pomade is great for getting separation and definition on the ends of hair. Plus it adds tons of shine."

"To smooth flyaways, I put a little bit of styling cream on the palms of my hands and lightly apply to my hair after it's in a ponytail. Do this during the day if little hairs start sticking out."

YOUR *pony* LOOK BOOK

HAYDEN PANETTIERE

Short hair *can* rock a pony! Use an elastic that matches your hair color for a seamless look.

GUCCI

Give a sleek pony some attitude with a trendy feather hair extension and some crimp.

WHITNEY PORT

Try a classic high ponytail. After you tie your hair up, tug at the crown to create a flirty little bump.

MICHAEL KORS

Unleash your artsy side by weaving fabric or ribbon randomly through your hair. The result: a messy masterpiece.

BEYONCÉ

A wavy side pony looks extraflirty when you add a soft swoop in front.

DONNA KARAN

Snap up all the attention with a quirky hair cuff and a mile-long ponytail. (You can fake extra length with extensions.)

Get inspired by these celeb and runway looks— the possibilities are endless!

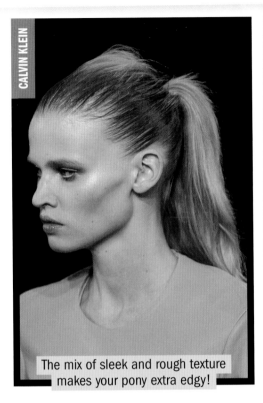

CALVIN KLEIN

The mix of sleek and rough texture makes your pony extra edgy!

CAROLINA HERRERA

Just for fun, make a loop with your pony, tucking the ends back into the base. Wrap a section of hair around the band and secure with a pin.

HAILEE STEINFELD

A great way to recycle day-old curls: Spritz them with a shine spray, then pull your hair into a ladylike side pony.

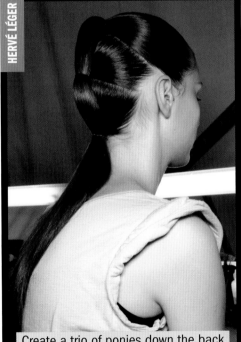

HERVÉ LÉGER

Create a trio of ponies down the back of your head and get triple the impact!

NINA DOBREV

Ponytails don't have to be sleek and smooth. Gather up all your spirals loosely into a high pony for a flirty, girly vibe!

PROENZA SCHOULER

It's the ponytail version of sexy bedhead: Make a super-loose pony, then tug out some hair above and below the elastic.

VOLUMIZING MOUSSE

A large squirt gives you an **ultra-voluminous effect**!

BLOW-DRYER NOZZLE

Use it to target the airflow for a **sleek, silky-smooth** updo!

STRONG-HOLD HAIRSPRAY

Your style **won't fall flat** when you spray this all over.

RATTAIL COMB

Easily allows you to **back-comb** your hair at the roots to bring your style to new heights.

BOBBY PINS

Need to use a lot of pins? Go with the kind that match your hair color to **discreetly secure** your do.

updos & buns

Step up your updo with fun embellishments and personal touches—it's easy to make these classic styles modern and cool. You'll take your look to new heights!

JEWELED BOBBY PIN

Adds an extraspecial **sparkly touch**!

LARGE-BARREL CURLING IRON

Gives you the **perfect volume** and texture.

ULTIMATE updos & buns

These four fun looks will take you anywhere!

STEP 1:
Create a **part across the top** of your head from one ear to the other and **clip the front section** out of the way.

STEP 2:
Grab a couple of **brightly colored clip-in extensions** and snap them into your hair at the part, leaving a few inches between them.

STEP 3:
Apply a little **gel** to your sides, then pull your hair up into a **midheight ponytail,** leaving a small section out in the back. Tie the tail with an **elastic,** then wrap the piece of hair around the base to cover it and **pin.**

STEP 4:
If your hair is long, **loosely braid the tail,** then fold it under and pin to make a casual loop. Got shorter hair? Just do a simple bun.

school

Lace your braid with your school colors (or match your outfit) for a playful twist.

STEP 1:

Apply a **straightening balm** to damp hair from roots to ends, then blow-dry it in sections with a **paddle brush** to get it super-smooth.

STEP 2:

Gather your hair into a **loose ponytail** and secure it with an elastic at your crown, then wrap your hair into a messy bun.

STEP 3:

Gently tug at the hair around your bun to loosen it. Slip on a **colorful skinny headband,** and add another one slightly behind the first one. Finish with a mist of hairspray.

weekend

Double pastel headbands make this chic bun super-playful.

STEP 1:

Rub a small amount of **pomade** between your hands, then smooth over dry hair to **tone down frizz.**

STEP 2:

Loosely twist one side of your hair, then **gather the twist** and the rest of your hair to make a bun. Let pieces fall against your face for a perfectly imperfect effect.

STEP 3:

Take **a spin pin** and insert from the top of the bun, twisting it in to secure tightly. Insert another at the base.

date

For a softer take on the classic chignon, try a freestyle knot—and leave out some romantic face-framing pieces.

STEP 1:
Apply **smoothing cream** to damp hair and blow-dry it straight for a sleek starting point.

STEP 2:
Make a **ponytail on top of your head** so that it sits either more to the left or to the right—not smack-dab in the middle. Secure it with two elastics, one on top of the other, for extra height.

STEP 3:
Wrap the tail around the base to create the bun, **tuck the ends under,** and stick in a few pins for hold.

17 TIP:
Shine on! Add a touch of shine spray to your overall look to play up the sleekness.

party

An off-center, wispy bun is the perfect mix of fun and fashion. Bonus: It's fuss-free!

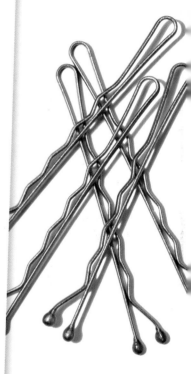

TOP updos & buns

Try these tricks from Hollywood's top stylists!

SECRETS

1 SKIP THE BLOWOUT!

"The best way to make an updo look modern is to keep some of the natural texture in the hair—in other words, don't make it perfectly straight before you pull it up. Movement and softness keep the style from looking too contrived."
–Charles Baker Strahan

Whitney Port

2 FIGHT FRIZZ!

"When wearing your hair in a high, tight bun, tame baby hairs around your face by spritzing hairspray onto a toothbrush and brushing your hair back." **–Jenny Cho**

Leighton Meester

Selena Gomez

3 PICK THE PERFECT PINS!

"If your hair is shoulder length or slightly longer, bobby pins will secure your updo. For girls who have long hair—especially if it's thick—big, U-shaped hairpins are best. They'll hold your hair better."
–Christian Marc

Lea Michele

4 STYLE SECOND-DAY HAIR!

"I don't like to create updos on freshly washed hair. When it's too clean, it doesn't hold the style as well. The day after or two days after washing is always best."
–Christian Marc

Jamie Chung

5 GET A GOOD GRIP!

"If you crisscross bobby pins into an X, that really holds the hair in place. When I'm doing a tight bun, I'll secure it with four Xs." **–Mark Townsend**

seventeen
BEAUTY SMARTIES

Megan

AGE: 16

HOMETOWN: Austin, TX

STAR SIGN: Libra

FAVE COLOR: Yellow

HOBBIES: Sailing, shopping, reading magazines

> **I feel the prettiest when my hair is sleek and out of my face. I love pulling it back to show off my makeup or accessories!**

✳ See Megan create this look at seventeen.com/beautysmarties.

MY BEST TIP

"Always use a **mirror** to check the back of your hair before you go out. It sounds silly, but people will see your hair from all angles!"

MY GO-TO PROM STYLE

"Braiding or **weaving a ribbon** through an updo adds an **unexpected twist of texture and interest,** but it's simple so it still allows your dress to be the focal point."

A LOOK I LOVE

"The **gorgeous rolled updo** from the Chanel runway show was so unique and classy but simple to re-create."

my inspirations

MY CELEB CRUSH

"I love **Carrie Underwood**'s sweet, feminine updos with face-framing curls. She reminds me of a modern-day princess. She is so elegant."

MY GO-TO ACCESSORY

"**Embellished headbands** to make a statement! I've made headbands with jewels, lace, and flowers—they each add something special to an outfit."

MY ESSENTIAL TOOL

"I love a **clipless curling wand**! It's easy to use and creates tight curls that add glamour to my updos."

Megan's look:
TOUSLED TOPKNOT

"The key to creating this look is to let the style get a little messy! The texture makes it look playful and sweet."

LIFT

"Using just your hands, **rake the front of hair to one side** (to get the soft swirl), then loosely pull your hair up into a **high ponytail** and tie it with an **elastic band**."

WIND

"**Wrap the length of the pony around** the base of the elastic (be sure to leave a piece of hair out in the back for the braid). **Tuck in a few hairpins around the base** to keep it in place."

SHAPE

"**Braid** the piece of hair you left out and **wrap it around** the base of the bun. Secure with **U-shaped pins.** Finish with a spritz of **hairspray** all over for hold."

"My hair is straight, so I have to spray it all over with texturizing spray to make sure my updos will hold."

"A paddle brush is great for teasing and creating a slightly disheveled texture."

"These pins are the best for updos because they stay hidden in the hair."

YOUR updos & buns

ASHLEY GREENE

To add subtle sexiness to a basic chignon, make a deep side part and let the front of your hair swoop down across your forehead before creating the bun.

LUCY HALE

For a fresh take on a bun, create a center part and pull out some wavy face-framing pieces.

FENDI

An unstructured updo becomes even cooler with a fashion-forward, spiky headband.

LUCA LUCA

Make a bun edgier by using a row of bobby pins to keep your hair slicked back.

AMBER RILEY

Defined coils with height give short hair a dramatic flair!

MILEY CYRUS

Finger-comb your hair and use just your hands to smooth it back for an effortless, almost slept-in effect.

LOOK BOOK

Get inspired by these celeb and runway looks—the possibilities are endless!

MARNI

Just pin up the back of your hair and let the front hang loose.

KAT GRAHAM

You can't go wrong with a classic ballerina bun—it's a chic look for day or night.

CHLOË GRACE MORETZ

To get a cool high pony, tuck and pin the ends of the tail under.

ZENDAYA

A trick for an easier updo: Bend over while you pull your hair up on top of your head.

HAILEE STEINFELD

Be shamelessly glam and rock a sleek topknot with a glitzy headband.

RIHANNA

A good hairspray is the key to a Bardot-inspired bump that won't collapse. Spray it on generously!

YOUR ULTIMATE beauty resource guide

customize *your* look

The key to looking great every day? Knowing what works for *your* unique features. It's all about playing up your skin tone and bringing out the best parts of your hair texture—master that and you'll learn to love what you've got!

the best shades for

fair

Porcelain skin has rosy undertones, so choose a **pink-based foundation.** You look great in cool makeup shades like petal pink, soft lilac, icy metallics, and bright, blue-based red lipsticks.

beige

Foundations with a tinge of yellow really flatter you. For color, opt for warm tones like peachy pinks, nudes, taupes, and earthy neutrals. Feeling bold? Rock a vibrant orange lipstick.

golden

Makeup that's **yellow, peach, or gold-based** harmonizes well with your skin tone. Play with coral and melon colors, honey-beiges, and olive greens. Like brights? Try violet shadow or fuchsia gloss with golden shimmer.

your skin tone!

olive

You need a **golden-toned foundation,** but your versatile complexion can pull off a range of makeup shades, from pastels to earthy metallics to vivid, tropical colors like teal and tangerine.

bronze

Rich, caramel-colored foundation blends right into your warm skin tone. Make golden nudes, coppers, and rusts your go-to colors, and experiment with dramatic pinks, brick reds, and plums.

deep

If you look good in silver, go with **blue-based foundation;** try **orange-based coverage** if you look better in gold. Intense shades like burgundy, forest green, and spicy hues pop against dark complexions.

the right products for

relaxed

YOUR MUST-HAVES:

strengthening shampoo and conditioner: To rebuild fragile, chemically straightened hair, try products with proteins and oils.

heat protector: Spritz one on before heat styling to avoid breakage.

protein mask: When your hair feels weak or looks limp, an intense conditioner will help bring it back to life.

straight

YOUR MUST-HAVES:

volumizing shampoo and conditioner: Body-boosting products will keep your strands from falling flat.

thickening lotion: For even more volume, apply it to freshly washed hair before you blow-dry it.

dry shampoo: Use it to revive greasy roots in between wash days.

wavy

YOUR MUST-HAVES:

lightweight shampoo and conditioner: Products that are hydrating but not too heavy will keep your waves from drooping.

leave-in conditioner: It's a daily essential for soft, touchable waves.

beach spray: Scrunch it onto damp hair and air-dry to add sexy, effortless texture.

your hair texture!

curly

YOUR MUST-HAVES:

moisturizing shampoo and conditioner: Your hair tends to be thirsty—quench it with rich, creamy products.

curl-shaping cream: For springy, defined curls, rake it through wet hair with your fingers.

antifrizz serum: Mix it with curling cream to keep flyaways under control.

super-curly

YOUR MUST-HAVES:

sulfate-free shampoo and conditioner: They won't strip out much-needed moisture from your hair.

wide-tooth comb: To gently detangle, use it in the shower while your hair is wet.

glossing spray: Apply it before diffusing damp curls for a pretty shine.

SKIN

You feel so confident when your skin is clear, soft, and flawless. Thankfully, getting it that way is easy: Just follow our customized advice and it's yours.

FIND YOUR perfect

17 TIP:

Make your mask multitask! Dab a little bit onto blemishes and leave it on overnight to treat problem spots while you snooze.

CLEANSE

When your skin gets slick, lather up with a face wash that contains **salicylic acid**—it'll get rid of the gunk in your pores that leads to acne.

MOISTURIZE

Skipping moisturizer can actually make your face greasier (your skin will produce more oil if it's too dry). To give skin a shot of moisture minus the excess grease, use a **mattifying oil-free lotion.**

TREAT

Clear up pesky pimples with a **pore-refining mask made with sulfur,** a great (and speedy!) acne-fighting ingredient.

oily

If you've got large pores, excess shine, and frequent breakouts, keep your face clear with oil-zapping products that won't strip your skin.

skin ROUTINE

dry

CLEANSE
The key is to wash away dirt and makeup without robbing skin of natural oils. A gentle, **soap-free wash** is your best bet.

17 TIP:
Cucumbers have a hydrating effect—use them around your eyes to nourish the delicate, dry skin around that area.

MOISTURIZE
Hydrate your face with a **nourishing moisturizer infused with hyaluronic acid** to help hold moisture in your skin.

TREAT
Thirsty skin can look dull or sallow—add an **intense moisturizing mask** to your weekly routine to bring out radiance. Scan the label for nourishing ingredients like **aloe or vitamin E.**

Your biggest complexion concerns are fighting flakes, dullness, and uncomfortable tightness. You need to restore hydration and give your skin a healthy-looking glow.

CLEANSE

Go for a **mild face-wash formula** that contains glycolic acid or soy to free the dirt that's stuck in your pores—it won't suck your skin dry.

MOISTURIZE

A lotion with a **light-weight texture** will do wonders for those patches of dryness that usually pop up on your cheeks—without the risk of breakouts.

TREAT

When you get the greasies on your T-zone, swipe it with a **shine-controlling toner** or whip out some **oil-blotting papers** to discreetly sop up oil anytime, anywhere.

combo

Some areas are taut and dry—while other spots look like you slathered them with oil! Choose products that'll bring back the balance but aren't too harsh.

MOISTURIZE

Your moisturizer should contain pampering ingredients like **oatmeal for itch relief or chamomile to tone down redness** while boosting hydration. Other skin-calmers to embrace: **green tea, lavender, and shea butter.**

CLEANSE

A **milky wipe-off cleanser** or a **thick, creamy wash** will whisk away makeup and grime. Look for a formula that's **fragrance-free** and **noncomedogenic,** and wash your face only at night.

TREAT

Keep the less-is-more rule in mind when using **face scrubs and masks**—use them no more than once a week to avoid upsetting your skin.

sensitive

Harsh weather, the wrong product, and even stress can cause redness, blotchiness, or stinging. Be sure to stick with gentle formulas that help calm and soothe irritable skin.

FIGHT acne

Zits don't stand a chance against these foolproof tips.

How to Treat...

Blackheads

Wash morning and night with a **salicylic acid–infused cleanser** to deep-clean pores. Apply a **pimple-fighting mask** in the shower once a week—the warmth and steam will help open up clogged pores.

Inflamed Whiteheads

A face wash with **glycolic acid** is your best defense against breakouts—it helps speed up cell turnover and destroys the bacteria that can build up during your sleep. Once a week, add an **exfoliating scrub** to your regimen to slough away flakes, dirt, and grease.

Cystic, Underground Zits

The type of bacteria that's causing your painful, swollen flare-ups needs a cleanser that contains **2% beta hydroxy acid**—use it in the morning and before bed. When monster zits pop up, dab on a **spot treatment** and leave it on overnight to reduce the swelling.

3 biggest acne myths

Myth #1: Chocolate and fried foods can aggravate acne.

Nope. It's the combo of oil and bacteria that brings on blemishes—not what you eat.

Myth #2: Alcohol is a good treatment for pimple-prone skin.

Wrong! Benzoyl peroxide and salicylic acid are best for zapping breakouts. The overly drying effect of alcohol will only cause your skin to ooze more oil and create more zits.

Myth #3: Acne-prone skin should be scrubbed extra hard.

Not true. Exfoliating too aggressively or too often irritates the skin and makes it more likely to form pimples. So be gentle!

Cover your pimples the right way!

1 PREP

Dot a **primer** that has acne-fighting ingredients onto the spots you want to camouflage to help relieve swelling while you hide them.

2 SMOOTH

Apply **concealer** with a flat, stiff brush for better control. Don't forget to blend—a thick blob of makeup will call attention to the pimple.

3 SET

Dust **translucent powder** over your concealer to make it last all day without getting cakey.

BE smooth

legs

DO USE A RAZOR WITH MOISTURIZING STRIPS to protect skin from cuts and irritation. Start shaving at the end of your shower to give the water time to **soften the hairs**—you'll get silkier, bump-free results.

DON'T SHY AWAY FROM DEPILATORIES. The newer formulas work quickly, are easier to apply, and they don't smell bad!

underarms

DO PROTECT YOUR PITS WITH A MOISTURIZING DEODORANT. The delicate skin can get irritated from shaving or waxing, so pamper it with a **nourishing solid formula.**

DON'T FORGET TO EXFOLIATE BEFORE YOU SHAVE. Sloughing will help stop excess **dead skin cells** from building up and causing discoloration.

ALL OVER

Hair removal is a snap with these easy defuzzing tips!

face

DO FOLLOW THE DIRECTIONS ON THE BACK OF YOUR FACIAL-HAIR REMOVAL CREAM carefully to **avoid any mishaps** that might occur from leaving it on too long or applying it incorrectly.

DON'T WAX OR DISSOLVE HAIR ON YOUR UPPER LIP RIGHT BEFORE A BIG NIGHT OUT. It's best to **remove hair a few days prior to an event** just in case you get irritation that needs time to heal.

bikini

DO MAKE SURE TO USE A FRESH RAZOR to keep your fragile bikini line **safe from nicks.** If shaving causes bumps to surface the next day, ditch the blade—a pro waxing session at a reputable salon is likely better for your skin.

DON'T SET YOURSELF UP FOR INGROWN HAIRS! Exfoliate with a **body scrub** or a wet washcloth in between waxing appointments to prevent new hairs from getting stuck under layers of dead skin.

169

GET A FAUX glow

Pick your formula!

SPRAY
Mist it onto tricky-to-reach areas, like your back.

TOWELETTES
They're presoaked with the perfect amount of tanner for goofproof results. Bonus: They're travel-friendly!

LOTION
It's usually tinted, so you can catch spots you skipped before it's too late!

MOUSSE
The lightweight texture is great for layering if you want a darker tan.

GEL
Delivers a fast hint of color that washes off easily.

GRADUAL
Great for self-tan newbies—the subtle color builds up over a few days.

17 TIP:
Stay dry! Give your self-tanner a few hours to set before you work out, shower, or head out into humid weather. If the product gets wet too soon, it'll streak.

These essential tips will get you a goddesslike bronze every time (without the damaging effects of the sun or the dangers of a tanning booth)!

1. Exfoliate

Mix a few drops of water with a body scrub and rub it over your skin while it's dry. Layers of old cells can get in the way of your tanner, causing embarrassing uneven patches. Rinse your skin.

2. Moisturize

The drier your skin is, the more self-tanner will cling to it, resulting in too-deep, unnatural color. Avoid heading into orange territory by applying a generous dose of body lotion to the areas you want to tan.

3. Apply

Certain areas of the skin absorb tanner more easily than others. A makeup sponge can help smoothly blend a thin amount over tricky parts like ankles, knees, elbows, and face. When you're done, clean the excess off hands, knees, and elbows with self-tan-remover wipes.

nails

Whether you're feeling wild, quirky, or low-key, top off your look with a manicure that matches your mood.

MASTER A mani

Get flawless fingers with these must-have tools!

shape

smooth

DUAL-SIDED FILE
Use the rougher side for **shaping;** rub the smoother side on tops of nails to **buff away ridges.**

CUTICLE PUSHER
Push your cuticles back with a **stainless steel** cuticle pusher (it won't harbor bacteria like the wooden ones!).

GLITTER
While your top coat is **still slightly wet,** carefully press glitter onto nails.

CUTICLE OIL
It **amps up shine** and keeps skin soft!

CLIPPERS
Snip nails in **tiny sections** to avoid breaking and splitting.

BRUSH
Choose a nail brush with **natural bristles;** use it to gently scrub your nails with soap and water.

POLISH
For a **longer-lasting mani,** let each coat dry before applying the next.

POLISH REMOVER
A nourishing non-acetone formula with **vitamin E** is easier on your nails.

HOW-TO:

1 SHAPE

Run a **fine-grit emery board** across your nails in a back-and-forth motion. When they're evened out, round the edges a bit to keep them from snagging.

2 PREP

Soak your nails in soapy water for five minutes to soften the cuticles, then gently nudge them back with an orange stick. Don't have a cuticle pusher? Use a towel or washcloth. Once cuticles are neat, **apply hand lotion,** then wipe off your nail beds.

3 POLISH

Apply a base coat to protect nails from stains, then do **two thin coats of nail lacquer.** Finish with a **clear top coat** and let it dry fully. Reapply your top coat every other day for a mani that lasts.

CREATE A PERFECT pedi

Here are all the tips you'll need for sandal-ready feet!

HOW-TO:

1 SOFTEN

Soak your feet in warm water for 10 minutes. Use a **pumice stone** or callus remover to smooth off rough skin from heels and toes. Rinse thoroughly and pat dry. Follow with a **moisturizing lotion.**

2 FILE

Trim nails with a **toenail clipper,** then round the edges with a file to create a "squoval" shape. Snip off any dead skin from the sides, then swipe nails with **polish remover** to whisk away excess oil.

3 PAINT

For a smooth surface, apply a **base coat,** then layer on **two thin coats of color.** When dry to the touch, apply a protective clear **top coat.** Let dry completely and rub on some cuticle oil for extra shine.

CUTICLE NIPPER

The **precise tip** is perfect for safely snipping pesky hangnails!

TOE SEPARATOR

Helps **prevent smudges** while you DIY!

POINTED COTTON SWABS

Use them to **clean underneath nails** or to fix any mistakes!

COTTON BALLS

Press a remover-soaked ball against your nails for 10 seconds, then slide it off—you'll have **dissolved the polish** a bit and it will come off more easily.

PUMICE STONE

Use a pumice stone (it's a type of lava!) to **gently exfoliate** rough spots on feet.

FOOT SCRUB

Don't let cracked heels ruin your pedi! **Slough skin** in the shower two to three times a week.

INSPIRATION: *best colors*

Get your hands on one of these cute hues!

1 CLASSIC!

A true red always looks chic, and it's easier to wear than you think—the timeless hue is not too orangy or too deep.

2 BRIGHT!

Punchy, happy nail color can instantly put you in a good mood! Experiment with hot pinks—they're feminine and fun.

Emma Roberts

Zendaya

3 PALE!

When you want subtle impact, go with a pastel or nude shade. Neutrals are not only versatile and modern, but they also make your fingers look longer!

4 DARK!

Almost-black shades add sexy intensity and sophistication to your look. Try them for a big night out (or when you want to show some edge)!

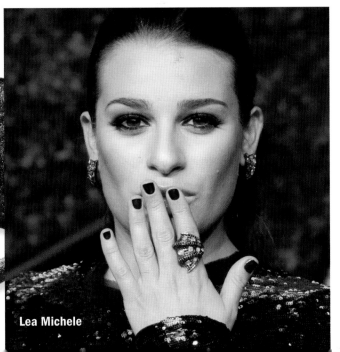

Lea Michele

5 DARING!

You'll have no trouble getting attention with playful, unexpected nails. Can't decide on a color? Paint one nail on each hand in a contrasting shade.

INSPIRATION: *fun patterns*

Add personality to your nails with a trendy detail or texture!

1 FUN STICKERS!

Give nails a partly girly, partly rock-and-roll feel with these playful stickers. They're even better with a layer of sheer shimmer color over them!

Katy Perry

2 GRAPHIC DRAWINGS!

Draw a crazy pattern on your nails with a nail art pen (it takes a plain color up a few notches)!

Naya Rivera

3
PRINTED PRESS-ONS!

With these nail-shaped adhesive patterns, you literally just press on a print—no artistic talent required!

4
CUTE TATTOOS!

Mix and match sticky tattoos to create your own unique design!

5
SPARKLY STUDS!

Add glitz to your manicure with rhinestones. Stick them just along the tip of your nail or add jewels all over.

Special Occasion

Sometimes you want to look good—sometimes you want to look *wow*! Make a big event (whether it's your prom, Sweet Sixteen, or quinceañera) even more unforgettable with your prettiest makeup and most amazing hair ever. We'll show you how!

INSPIRATION: *makeup*

Focus on one standout detail and you'll be sure to turn heads!

1 MATTE RED LIPS!

Bold red with a polished finish is so simple and draws attention to your smile. Apply it with a tiny brush for more precision.

2 DOUBLE-LINED LIDS!

Mix a glittery liner with a bright one to give eyes a one-two glam punch.

Elie Saab Couture

3
FANCY LASHES!

Dramatic faux fringe will make your eyes look huge. Stick lashes on with black glue—it's neater.

4
SHIMMERING LIPS!

A sparkly gloss adds juicy dimension to your pout. Try a rosy pink shade to flatter your natural lip color.

Ralph Lauren

5
SHEER GLOW!

For a soft, pretty look, dust loose bronzer onto your cheeks and nose to catch the light. (That and a dramatic winged eye are all you need!)

INSPIRATION: *hair*

**The great thing about these notice-me looks:
You don't need a salon to do them!**

1 EMBELLISHED BUN!

Wrap a sequined headband around your updo to instantly dress it up!

Anna Sui

2 RETRO WAVES!

Use rollers to get loose curls, then pair them with a deep side part to create a sense of drama.

3
TWIRLED TOPKNOT!

A high, twisted bun looks chic set to one side. Spritz it with plenty of hairspray to keep it in place.

5
STATEMENT HEADBAND!

Whether you wear your hair up or down, a flashy headband is a gorgeous finishing touch.

4 BEJEWELED BRAID!

A pretty braid gets dressed up with sparkly pins dusted throughout.

PHOTO CREDITS

COVER
J Muckle.

FRONT MATTER
Page 1: J Muckle/Studio D.

Page 2: J Muckle/Studio D.

Page 4: Still Lifes (clockwise from top left): Jeffrey Westbrook/Studio D; J Muckle/Studio D (2); Jeffrey Westbrook/Studio D (3); Jeffrey Westbrook/Studio D.

Page 6: Perry Hagopian.

GIRLY
Pages 10-11: Still Lifes: J Muckle/Studio D.

Page 12: Real-Girl Photo: Chris Eckert/Studio D. Still Lifes (clockwise from top left): J Muckle/Studio D; Jesus Ayala/Studio D; J Muckle/Studio D.

Page 13: Main Photo: Ondrea Barbe. Still Lifes (clockwise from top left): Jesus Ayala/Studio D; Jeffrey Westbrook/Studio D; J Muckle/Studio D (2).

Page 14: Real-Girl Photo: Peter Rosa/Studio D. Still Lifes: J Muckle/Studio D.

Page 15: Real-Girl Photo: Ondrea Barbe. Still Lifes: J Muckle/Studio D.

Page 16: Still Lifes (clockwise from top left): J Muckle/Studio D; Jesus Ayala/Studio D; J Muckle/Studio D. Palmer: Jeffrey Mayer/WireImage. Jenner: Kyle Rover/Startraks.

Page 17: Still Lifes: J Muckle/Studio D. Moretz: Brian To/FilmMagic. Conrad: Jordan Strauss/WireImage. Collins: Joseph Kerlakian/Startraks.

Page 18: Peter Rosa/Studio D.

Page 19: Clockwise from top left: Moises de Pena/Getty Images; Getty Images; Jeffrey Westbrook/Studio D; J Muckle/Studio D; Courtesy of Sony Pictures Entertainment; C Squared Studios; J Muckle/Studio D.

Page 20: Peter Rosa/Studio D. Stylist: Andrew Mukamal. Hair: Ursula Stephen for Motions/Epiphany Artist Group. Makeup: Jordy at Bryan Bantry Agency using Diorshow.

Page 21: Real-Girl Photos: Peter Rosa Studio/D (3). Stylist: Andrew Mukamal. Hair: Ursula Stephen for Motions/Epiphany Artist Group. Makeup: Jordy at Bryan Bantry Agency using Diorshow. Still Lifes: J Muckle/Studio D.

Page 22: Clockwise from top left: Jordan Strauss/WireImage; Jason LeVeris/FilmMagic; Tony DiMaio/Startraks; Imaxtree; Michael Williams/Startraks; Imaxtree.

Page 23: Clockwise from top left: Imaxtree; Sara De Boer/Startraks; Imaxtree; Jeffrey Mayer/WireImage; Imaxtree; Justin Campbell/Startraks.

GLAM
Pages 24-25: Still Lifes (clockwise from top left): J Muckle/Studio D; Jeffrey Westbrook/Studio D; J Muckle/Studio D (2); Lara Robby/Studio D; Jeffrey Westbrook/Studio D.

Page 26: Main Photo: Juan Algarin. Still Lifes (clockwise from top left): Jeffrey Westbrook/Studio D; Devon Jarvis/Studio D; Jeffrey Westbrook/Studio D; Jeffrey Westbrook/Studio D; J Muckle/Studio D.

Page 27: Real-Girl Photo: Chris Eckert/Studio D. Still Lifes (clockwise from top left): J Muckle/Studio D (2); Philip Friedman/Studio D; Don Penny/Studio D.

Page 28: Real-Girl Photo: Peter Rosa/Studio D. Still Lifes (clockwise from top left): J Muckle/Studio D; Jeffrey Westbrook/Studio D; Chris Eckert/Studio D; Stuart Tyson/Studio D.

Page 29: Main Photo: Ondrea Barbe. Still Lifes (clockwise from top right): Kevin Sweeney/Studio D; Don Penny/Studio D; Jeffrey Westbrook/Studio D;

J Muckle/Studio D (2); Jeffrey Westbrook/Studio D.

Page 30: Still Lifes (clockwise from top right): Ylva Erevall/Studio D; J Muckle/Studio D (2). Benson: Paul Archuleta/FilmMagic. Thorne: Michael Buckner/Getty Images.

Page 31: Still Lifes (clockwise from top right): J Muckle/Studio D; Jesus Ayala/Studio D; Stuart Tyson/Studio D. Riley: Debbie Vanstory/Startraks. Meester: Rob Loud: WireImage. Ushkowitz: Jon Kopaloff/FilmMagic.

Page 32: Wendy Hope/Studio D.

Page 33: Still Lifes: (Lipstick, Polish) J Muckle/Studio D; (Jacket, Shoe) Jesus Ayala/Studio D; (Earrings) Kevin Sweeney/Studio D. Beyoncé: WENN.

Page 34: Chris Eckert/Studio D. Stylist: Andrew Mukamal. Hair: Riad Azar for TRESemmé at Opus Beauty. Makeup: Jordy Poon for Dior Beauty.

Page 35: Real-Girl Photos: Chris Eckert/Studio D (6). Stylist: Andrew Mukamal. Hair: Riad Azar for TRESemmé at Opus Beauty. Makeup: Jordy Poon for Dior Beauty. Still Lifes (clockwise from top right): Ylva Erevall/Studio D; J Muckle/Studio D (3).

Page 36: Clockwise from top left: Stephen Lovekin/Getty Images; Justin Campbell/Startraks; Mike Marsland/WireImage; Imaxtree; JB Lacroix/WireImage; Justin Campbell/Startraks.

Page 37: Clockwise from top left: Kyle Rover/Startraks; Mark Sullivan/WireImage; Imaxtree (2); Jordan Strauss/WireImage; Kyle Rover/Startraks.

CLASSIC
Pages 38-39: Still Lifes (clockwise from top left): J Muckle/Studio D; Jeffrey Westbrook/Studio D; J Muckle/Studio D (2); Lara Robby/Studio D; Jeffrey Westbrook/Studio D.

Page 40: Main Photo: Olivia Graham. Still Lifes (clockwise from top left): J Muckle/Studio D (3); Philip Friedman/Studio D (2).

Page 41: Real-Girl Photo: Peter Rosa/Studio D. Still Lifes (clockwise from top left): J Muckle/Studio D; Jeffrey Westbrook/Studio D; Chris Eckert/Studio D; J Muckle/Studio D.

Page 42: Main Photo: Sabine Liewald. Still Lifes (clockwise from top left): J Muckle/Studio D (2); Jesus Ayala/Studio D.

Page 43: Main Photo: Juan Algarin. Still Lifes (clockwise from top right): Jesus Ayala/Studio D; J Muckle/Studio D; Don Penny/Studio D.

Page 44: Still Lifes (from top): J Muckle/Studio D; Jeffrey Westbrook/Studio D. Gomez: Steve Granitz/WireImage. Swift: Michael Buckner/WireImage.

Page 45: Still Lifes: J Muckle/Studio D. Justice: Marion Curtis/Startraks. Zendaya: Albert Michael/Startraks. Seyfried: Amanda Schwab/Startraks.

Page 46: Peter Rosa/Studio D.

Page 47: Clockwise from top left: Imaxtree (3); John Kopaloff/FilmMagic; Samir Hussein/WireImage; J Muckle/Studio D; Richard Laird; Jesus Ayala/Studio D.

Page 48: Peter Rosa/Studio D. Stylist: Andrew Mukamal. Hair: Ursula Stephen for Motions/Epiphany Artist Group. Makeup: Jordy at Bryan Bantry Agency using Diorshow.

Page 49: Real-Girl Photos: Peter Rosa/Studio D (6). Stylist: Andrew Mukamal. Hair: Ursula Stephen for Motions/Epiphany Artist Group. Makeup: Jordy at Bryan Bantry Agency using Diorshow. Still Lifes (clockwise from top right): J Muckle/Studio D (3).

Page 50: Clockwise from top left: Jordan Strauss/WireImage; Imaxtree; Andy Kropa/Getty Images; Imaxtree; David Livingston/Getty Images; Imaxtree.

Page 51: Clockwise from top left: Steve Granitz/Getty Images; Albert Michael/Startraks; Imaxtree (2); Sara De Boer/Startraks; Charley Gallay/Getty Images.

EDGY
Pages 52-53: Still Lifes (clockwise from top left): J Muckle/Studio D (3); Jeffrey Westbrook/Studio D (2); Stuart Tyson/Studio D; J Muckle/Studio D.

Page 54: Main Photo: Anne Menke. Still Lifes (clockwise from top left): Jesus Ayala/Studio D; Jeffrey Westbrook/Studio D; J Muckle/Studio D (2).

Page 55: Real-Girl Photo: Peter Rosa/ Studio D. Still Lifes: J Muckle/Studio D.

Page 56: Real-Girl Photo: Wendy Hope/Studio D. Still Lifes: J Muckle/Studio D.

Page 57: Main Photo: Antoine Verglas. Still Lifes (clockwise from top right): J Muckle/Studio D; Jeffrey Westbrook/ Studio D; J Muckle/Studio D.

Page 58: Still Lifes (clockwise from top right): Jeffrey Westbrook/Studio D; Jesus Ayala/Studio D; Jeffrey Westbrook/ Studio D; J Muckle/Studio D. Lovato: Norman Scott/Startraks. Rihanna: Steve Granitz/WireImage.

Page 59: Still Lifes (clockwise from top): Kevin Sweeney/Studio D; J Muckle/ Studio D; Jeffrey Westbrook/Studio D (2). Perry: Dave Proctor/Startraks. Minaj: Theo Wargo/WireImage. Reed: Kevin Mazur/WireImage.

Page 60: Chris Eckert/Studio D.

Page 61: Still Lifes (clockwise from top left): Stuart Tyson/Studio D; J Muckle/ Studio D (2). Stefani: Mike Marsland/ WireImage. Runway Photo: Imaxtree.

Page 62: Peter Rosa Studio/D. Stylist: Andrew Mukamal. Hair: Riad Azar for TRESemmé at Opus Beauty. Makeup: Jordy for Bryan Bantry Agency.

Page 63: Real-Girl Photos: Peter Rosa/ Studio D (6). Stylist: Andrew Mukamal. Hair: Riad Azar for TRESemmé at Opus Beauty. Makeup: Jordy for Bryan Bantry Agency. Still Lifes: J Muckle/Studio D (2); Chris Eckert/Studio D; Jeffrey Westbrook.

Page 64: Clockwise from top left: Imaxtree (2); Stephen Lovekin/Getty Images; Julien Hekimian/WireImage; Imaxtree; Jon Kopaloff/FilmMagic.

Page 65: Clockwise from top left: Imaxtree; Kevin Mazur/WireImage; Ian Gavan/Getty Images; Frazer Harrison/Getty Images; Ferdaus Shamim/WireImage; Imaxtree.

BOHO

Pages 66–67: Clockwise from top left: J Muckle/Studio D (6); Jesus Ayala/ Studio D.

Page 68: Real-Girl Photo: Peter Rosa/ Studio D. Still Lifes: J Muckle/Studio D.

Page 69: Real-Girl Photo: Chris Eckert/Studio D. Still Lifes: (Mascara Swipe) Devon Jarvis/Studio D; (all others) J Muckle/Studio D.

Page 70: Real-Girl Photo: Chris Eckert/Studio D. Still Lifes: J Muckle/ Studio D.

Page 71: Main Photo: Olivia Graham. Still Lifes (clockwise from top right): Jesus Ayala/Studio D; J Muckle/ Studio D (4).

Page 72: Still Lifes: J Muckle/Studio D. Jenner: Albert Michael/Startraks. Fanning: Bill Davila/Startraks.

Page 73: Still Lifes: J Muckle/ Studio D. Kravitz: Steven Lovekin/ Getty Images. Port: Amanda Schwab/ Getty Images. Mitchell: Jason LaVeris/ FilmMagic.

Page 74: Peter Rosa/Studio D.

Page 75: Clockwise from top left: Rob Lang; J Muckle/Studio D; Jeffrey Westbook/Studio D; Charlotte Jenks Lewis/Studio D; Jamie McCarthy/ WireImage; J Muckle/Studio D.

Page 76: Peter Rosa Studio/D. Stylist: Andrew Mukamal. Hair: Riad Azar for TRESemmé at Opus Beauty. Makeup: Jordy for Bryan Bantry Agency.

Page 77: Real-Girl Photos: Peter Rosa Studio/D (4). Stylist: Andrew Mukamal. Hair: Riad Azar for TRESemmé at Opus Beauty. Makeup: Jordy for Bryan Bantry Agency. Still Lifes (from top): J Muckle/ Studio D; David Cook/Studio D; J Muckle/Studio D.

Page 78: Clockwise from top left: Imaxtree; Amanda Schwab/Getty Images; Imaxtree; Bill Davila/ Startraks; Amanda Schwab/Getty Images; Imaxtree.

Page 79: Clockwise from top left: Imaxtree; Sara De Boer/Startraks; Imaxtree; Jordan Strauss/WireImage; Tony DiMaio/Startraks; Imaxtree.

WAVES & CURLS

Page 82: Main Photo: Ondrea Barbe. Still Lifes (clockwise from top left): Marko Metzinger/Studio D; J Muckle/ Studio D.

Page 83: Main Photo: Ondrea Barbe. Still Lifes (clockwise from top left): J Muckle/Studio D (2); Chris Eckert/ Studio D.

Page 84: Main Photo: Peter Rosa/ Studio D. Still Lifes (clockwise from top right): J Muckle/Studio D (2); Jeffrey Westbrook/Studio D.

Page 85: Main Photo: Ondrea Barbe. Still Lifes (clockwise from top right): J Muckle/Studio D; Marko Metzinger/ Studio D.

Page 86: Main Photo: Ondrea Barbe. Still Lifes (clockwise from top left): J Muckle/Studio D (3); Jeffrey Westbrook/Studio D.

Page 87: Real-Girl Photo: Chris Eckert/Studio D. Still Lifes: J Muckle/ Studio D.

Page 88: Still Lifes (clockwise from top left): Jesus Ayala/Studio D; J Muckle/Studio D. Stone: Jon Kopaloff/FilmMagic. Michalka: Michael Tran/FilmMagic.

Page 89: Still Lifes: J Muckle/Studio D. Cosgrove: Jon Kopaloff/FilmMagic. Reed: Steve Granitz/WireImage. Rihanna: Nick Sadler/Startraks.

Page 90: Peter Rosa/Studio D.

Page 91: Clockwise from top left: J Muckle/Studio D; Gene Kornman/ John Kobal Foundation/Getty Images; J Muckle/Studio D; Imaxtree; J Muckle/Studio D; George Pimentel/ WireImage.

Page 92: Peter Rosa/Studio D. Stylist: Andrew Mukamal. Hair: Riad Azar for TRESemmé at Opus Beauty. Makeup: Jordy for Bryan Bantry Agency.

Page 93: Real-Girl Photos: Peter Rosa/Studio D (3). Stylist: Andrew Mukamal. Hair: Riad Azar for TRESemmé at Opus Beauty.

Makeup: Jordy for Bryan Bantry Agency. Still Lifes (from left): David Turner/ Studio D; Greg Marino/Studio D; Philip Friedman/Studio D.

Page 94: Clockwise from top left: Albert Michael/Startraks; Kevin Winter/Getty Images; Arnold Turner/ WireImage; Imaxtree; Kevin Mazur/ WireImage; Kyle Rover/Startraks.

Page 95: Clockwise from top left: Imaxtree; Tony DiMaio/Startraks; Imaxtree; Kyle Rover/Startraks; Jean Baptiste Lacroix/WireImage; Sara De Boer/Startraks.

BRAIDS & TWISTS

Page 96: Main Photos (from left): Peter Rosa/Studio D; Olivia Graham. Still Lifes: J Muckle/Studio D.

Page 97: Main Photo: Olivia Graham. Still Lifes: J Muckle/Studio D.

Page 98: Main Photo: Ondrea Barbe. Still Lifes (clockwise from top left): David Cook/Studio D; Ben Goldstein/ Studio D; J Muckle/Studio D; Jeffrey Westbook/Studio D.

Page 99: Main Photo: Olivia Graham. Still Lifes: J Muckle/Studio D.

Page 100: Main Photo: Chris Eckert/ Studio D. Still Lifes (clockwise from top left): Stuart Tyson/Studio D; J Muckle/ Studio D (2).

Page 101: Main Photo: Ondrea Barbe. Still Lifes: J Muckle/Studio D.

Page 102: Still Lifes: J Muckle/Studio D. Hudgens: Jason Merritt/FilmMagic. Olsen: Tommaso Boddi/WireImage.

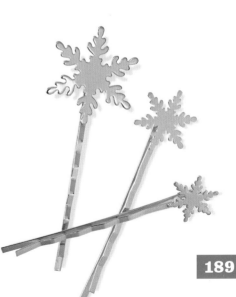

SLEEK

Page 110: Main Photo: Ondrea Barbe. Still Lifes (clockwise from top right): J Muckle/Studio D; Don Penny/ Studio D; Jeffrey Westbrook/Studio D; J Muckle/Studio D.

Page 111: Real-Girl Photo: Chris Eckert/Studio D. Still Lifes (clockwise from top left): J Muckle/Studio D; Daniel Hurst; J Muckle/Studio D.

Page 112: Real-Girl Photo: Chris Eckert/Studio D. Still Lifes: J Muckle/ Studio D.

Page 113: Real-Girl Photo: Chris Eckert/Studio D. Still Lifes: J Muckle/ Studio D.

Page 114: Real-Girl Photo: Ondrea Barbe. Still Lifes (clockwise from top left): Chris Eckert/Studio D; Richard Majchrzak/Studio D; J Muckle/Studio D (2).

Page 115: Chris Eckert/Studio D. Still Lifes: J Muckle/Studio D.

Page 116: Still Lifes (from left): J Muckle/Studio D; Chris Eckert/ Studio D. Conrad: Michael Williams/ Startraks. Szohr: Bill Davila/ Startraks.

Page 117: Still Lifes (from left): Jesus Ayala/Studio D; J Muckle/Studio D. Zendaya: Sara De Boer/Startraks. Stewart: Michael Williams/Startraks. Fanning: Jessie Grant/WireImage.

Page 118: Peter Rosa/Studio D.

Page 119: Clockwise from top left: Hulton Archive/Getty Images; Chris Eckert/Studio D; Don Penny/Studio D; J Muckle/Studio D; Jeff Kravitz/ FilmMagic; Norman Scott/Startraks.

Page 120: Peter Rosa/Studio D. Stylist: Andrew Mukamal. Hair: Riad Azar for TRESemmé at Opus Beauty. Makeup: Jordy at Bryan Bantry Agency using Diorshow.

Page 121: Real-Girl Photos: Peter Rosa/Studio D (3). Stylist: Andrew Mukamal. Hair: Riad Azar for TRESemmé at Opus Beauty. Makeup: Jordy at Bryan Bantry Agency using Diorshow. Still Lifes (clockwise from top right): J Muckle/Studio D (2); Greg Marino/Studio D.

Page 103: Still Lifes (from top): J Muckle/Studio D; Charlotte Jenks Lewis/Studio D. Agron: Jeffrey Mayer/ WireImage. Dobrev: Michael Tran/ FilmMagic. Thorne: Jason Merritt/ FilmMagic.

Page 104: Peter Rosa/Studio D.

Page 105: Clockwise from top left: Kevin Mazur/WireImage; Jen Lowery/ Startraks; Bill Davila/Startraks; Rosemary Calvert; Medioimages/ Photodisc; Christopher Coppola/ Studio D; Frazer Harrison/Getty Images for TRESemmé; J Muckle/Studio D.

Page 106: Peter Rosa/Studio D. Stylist: Andrew Mukamal. Hair: Ursula Stephen for Motions/Epiphany Artist Group. Makeup: Jordy at Bryan Bantry Agency using Diorshow.

Page 107: Real-Girl Photos: Peter Rosa/Studio D (3). Stylist: Andrew Mukamal. Hair: Ursula Stephen for Motions/Epiphany Artist Group. Makeup: Jordy at Bryan Bantry Agency using Diorshow. Still Lifes (clockwise from top right): Stuart Tyson/Studio D; Marko Metzinger/Studio D; J Muckle/ Studio D (2).

Page 108: Clockwise from top left: Kevin Mazur/WireImage; Kyle Rover/ Startraks; Imaxtree; Toni DiMaio/ Startraks; Seth Browarnik/Startraks; Albert Michael/Startraks.

Page 109: Clockwise from top left: Toni DiMaio/Startraks; Bill Davila/Startraks; Imaxtree; Sara De Boer/Startraks (2); Daniel Boczarski/Getty Images.

Page 122: Clockwise from top left: Imaxtree; Sara De Boer/Startraks; Jon Kopaloff/FilmMagic; Imaxtree; Munawar Hosain/Startraks; Jerritt Clark/WireImage.

Page 123: Clockwise from top left: Michael Williams/Startraks; Imaxtree; Valerie Macon/Getty Images; Mike Marsland/WireImage; Alexandra Wyman/WireImage; Imaxtree.

PONIES

Page 124: Real-Girl Photo: Peter Rosa/Studio D. Still Lifes (clockwise from top right): J Muckle/Studio D; Jeffrey Westbrook/Studio D; Jesus Ayala/Studio D.

Page 125: Real-Girl Photo: Peter Rosa/Studio D. Still Lifes (clockwise from top left): Jeffrey Westbrook/Studio D; Chris Eckert/Studio D; J Muckle/ Studio D; David Turner/Studio D.

Page 126: Main Photo: Kate Powers. Still Lifes (clockwise from top left): J Muckle/Studio D (2); David Turner/ Studio D.

Page 127: Real-Girl Photo: Chris Eckert/Studio D. Still Lifes (clockwise from top lcft): J Muckle/ Studio D; David Turner/Studio D; MISCELLANEOUSSTOCK/Alamy.

Page 128: Main Photo: Chris Eckert/Studio D. Still Lifes (clockwise from top right): J Muckle/Studio D; Jeffrey Westbrook/Studio D; J Muckle/ Studio D.

Page 129: Main Photo: Chris Eckert/ Studio D. Still Lifes (clockwise from top left): J Muckle/Studio D; Jeffrey Westbrook/Studio D; J Muckle/ Studio D.

Page 130: Still Lifes (from left): J Muckle/Studio D; Philip Friedman/ Studio D. Dobrev: Bill Davila/Startraks. Hough: Michael Williams/Startraks.

Page 131: Still Lifes (clockwise from top left): Don Penny/Studio D; J Muckle/Studio D. Graham: Jordan Strauss/WireImage. McCord: Jeff Kravitz/FilmMagic. Cyrus: Michael Tran/FilmMagic.

Page 132: Peter Rosa/Studio D.

Page 133: Clockwise from top left: Imaxtree; J Muckle/Studio D; Jon

Kopaloff/FilmMagic; David Turner/ Studio D; Kevin Sweeney/Studio D; J Muckle/Studio D.

Page 134: Peter Rosa/Studio D. Stylist: Andrew Mukamal. Hair: Ursula Stephen for Motions/Epiphany Artist Group. Makeup: Jordy at Bryan Bantry Agency using Diorshow.

Page 135: Real-Girl Photos: Peter Rosa/Studio D (3). Stylist: Andrew Mukamal. Hair: Ursula Stephen for Motions/Epiphany Artist Group. Makeup: Jordy at Bryan Bantry Agency using Diorshow. Still Lifes (from left): Devon Jarvis/Studio D; J Muckle/ Studio D (2).

Page 136: Clockwise from top left: Sara De Boer/Startraks; Imaxtree; Albert Michael/Startraks; Imaxtree; Jon Kopaloff/FilmMagic; Frazer Harrison/ Getty Images.

Page 137: Clockwise from top left: Frazer Harrison/Getty Images for Mercedes-Benz Fashion Week; Kyle Rover/Startraks; Imaxtree; George Pimental/WireImage; Imaxtree.

UPDOS & BUNS

Page 138: Real-Girl Photo: Peter Rosa/Studio D. Still Lifes (clockwise from top left): Chris Eckert/Studio D (2); J Muckle/Studio D (2).

Page 139: Main Photo: Sabine Liewald. Still Lifes (clockwise from top left): J Muckle/Studio D (2); Kevin Sweeney/Studio D.

Page 140: Real-Girl Photo: Chris Eckert/Studio D. Still Lifes: J Muckle/ Studio D.

Page 141: Real-Girl Photo: Sarra Fleur Abou-El-Haj/Studio D. Still Lifes: J Muckle/Studio D.

Page 142: Real-Girl Photos: Chris Eckert/Studio D (2). Still Lifes (clockwise from top left): J Muckle/ Studio D; Marko Metzinger/Studio D.

Page 143: Real-Girl Photo: Peter Rosa/Studio D. Still Lifes (clockwise from top left): J Muckle/Studio D (2); David Cook/Studio D; Marko Metzinger/Studio D.

Page 144: Still Life: Lara Robby/ Studio D. Meester: Jon Kopaloff/Film-Magic. Port: Marion Curtis/Startraks.

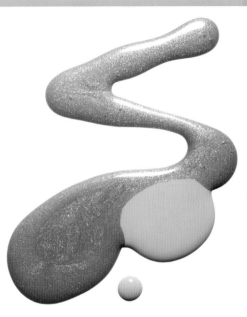

Page 145: Still Lifes: J Muckle/Studio D. Gomez and Michele: Steve Granitz/WireImage (2). Chung: Alberto E. Rodriguez/Getty Images.

Page 146: Chris Eckert/Studio D.

Page 147: Clockwise from top left: Fernanda Calfat/Getty Images; Judith Collins/Alamy; Imaxtree; Jeff Westbrook/Studio D; Jesus Ayala/Studio D; Ethan Miller/Getty Images.

Page 148: Peter Rosa/Studio D. Stylist: Andrew Mukamal. Hair: Riad Azar for TRESemmé at Opus Beauty. Makeup: Jordy at Bryan Bantry Agency using Diorshow.

Page 149: Real-Girl Photos: Peter Rosa/Studio D (3). Stylist: Andrew Mukamal. Hair: Riad Azar for TRESemmé at Opus Beauty. Makeup: Jordy at Bryan Bantry Agency using Diorshow. Still Lifes: J Muckle/Studio D.

Page 150: Clockwise from top left: Marion Curtis/Startraks; Tony DiMaio/Startraks; Imaxtree; Jon Kopaloff/WireImage; Steve Granitz/WireImage; Imaxtree.

Page 151: Clockwise from top left: Imaxtree; Tony DiMaio/Startraks; Nick Sadler/Startraks; Sara Jaye Weiss/Startraks; Kyle Rover/Startraks; David Livingston/Getty Images.

CUSTOMIZE YOUR LOOK

Page 154: Chris Craymer.

Page 155: Still Lifes (clockwise from top left): Jesus Ayala/Studio D; J Muckle/Studio D (5).

Page 156: Main Photos (from left): Wendy Hope/Studio D; Sarra Fleur Abou-El-Haj/Studio D; Chris Eckert/Studio D. Still Lifes (clockwise from top left): J Muckle/Studio D (4); Jeffrey Westbrook/Studio D; J Muckle/Studio D (2).

Page 157: Main Photos (from left): Peter Rosa/Studio D; Jeff Tse/Studio D; Peter Rosa/Studio D. Still Lifes (clockwise from top right): J Muckle/Studio D (5); Jeffrey Westbrook/Studio D (2); Jesus Ayala/Studio D; J Muckle/Studio D.

Page 158: Main Photos (from left): Sarra Fluer Abou-El-Haj/Studio D; Sarah Silver; Jeff Stephens. Still Lifes (clockwise from top right): J Muckle/Studio D (2); David Turner/Studio D; J Muckle/Studio D.

Page 159: Main Photos (from left): Chris Eckert/Studio D; Ondrea Barbe. Still Lifes (clockwise from top left): J Muckle/Studio D; Marko Metzinger/Studio D; J Muckle/Studio D (3).

SKIN

Page 160: Wendy Hope/Studio D.

Page 161: Still Lifes (clockwise from top left): J Muckle/Studio D; Devon Jarvis/Studio D; J Muckle/Studio D; Ylva Erevall/Studio D.

Page 162: Main Photo: Sarah McColgan. Still Lifes (clockwise from top right): J Muckle/Studio D; Devon Jarvis/Studio D; Chris Eckert/Studio D.

Page 163: Main Photo: Kate Powers. Still Lifes (clockwise from top left): Chris Eckert/Studio D; Ylva Erevall/Studio D; Greg Marino/Studio D.

Page 164: Main Photo: Peter Rosa/Studio D. Still Lifes (clockwise from top tight): J Muckle/Studio D; Jeffrey Westbrook/Studio D; J Muckle/Studio D.

Page 165: Main Photo: Sarah McColgan. Still Lifes (clockwise from top tight): Chris Eckert/Studio D; Stuart Tyson/Studio D; Lara Robby/Studio D.

Page 166: Main Photo: Sonja Pacho. Still Lifes: J Muckle/Studio D.

Page 167: Main Photos (from top): Akos; Sarah McColgan. Still Lifes (from left): J Muckle/Studio D (2); Chris Eckert/Studio D; Jeffrey Westbrook/Studio D.

Page 168: Main Photo: Olivia Graham. Still Lifes (from left): J Muckle/Studio D; Jesus Ayala/Studio D; J Muckle/Studio D.

Page 169: Main Photo: Olivia Graham. Still Lifes (from left): Jeffrey Westbrook/Studio D; David Turner/Studio D; Jesus Ayala/Studio D.

Page 170: Main Photo: Anne Menke. Still Lifes (clockwise from top left): Jesus Ayala/Studio D; J Muckle/Studio D; Stuart Tyson/Studio D; J Muckle/Studio D (2); Jeffrey Westbrook/Studio D; Chris Eckert/Studio D.

Page 171: Main Photo: Chris Craymer. Still Lifes (clockwise from top right): Chris Eckert/Studio D; J Muckle/Studio D.

NAILS

Page 172: Chris Eckert/Studio D.

Page 173: Still Life: Jeffrey Westbrook/Studio D.

Page 174: Still Lifes: (File) David Turner/Studio D; (Polishes) Jeffrey Westbrook/Studio D; (Cuticle Oil) Devon Jarvis/Studio D; (all others) J Muckle/Studio D.

Page 175: Main Photo: Akos. Still Lifes (from top): Stuart Tyson/Studio D; Jesus Ayala/Studio D.

Page 176: Main Photo: Kim Myers Robertson. Still Lifes (from top): J Muckle/Studio D (3); Charlotte Jenks Lewis/Studio D.

Page 177: Still Lifes (clockwise from top right): Chris Eckert/Studio D; J Muckle/Studio D; John Gollop/Alamy; Stuart Tyson/Studio D; Chris Eckert/Studio D; Jeffrey Westbrook/Studio D.

Page 178: Main Photos (from left): Donato Sardella/WireImage; Sarra Fleur Abou-El-Haj/Studio D. Still Lifes (from left): Jeff Harris; Jesus Ayala/Studio D.

Page 179: Main Photos (clockwise from top left): WireImage; Chris Eckert/Studio D; Jon Kopaloff/FilmMagic. Still Lifes (clockwise from top left): Jesus Ayala/Studio D; J Muckle/Studio D (3).

Page 180: Main Photos (from left): INF; Anne Menke. Still Lifes (clockwise from top left): Jesus Ayala/Studio D; J Muckle/Studio D.

Page 181: Main Photos (clockwise from top left): Chelsea Lauren/WireImage; Charles Masters; Peter Rosa/Studio D. Still Lifes (clockwise from top): J Muckle/Studio D (2); Jesus Ayala/Studio D.

SPECIAL OCCASION

Page 182: Terry Doyle.

Page 183: Still Lifes (clockwise from top left): Jesus Ayala/Studio D; J Muckle/Studio D (3).

Page 184: Main Photos (from left): Olivia Graham; Philippe Salomon. Still Lifes: J Muckle/Studio D.

Page 185: Main Photos (clockwise from top left): Imaxtree; Terry Doyle; Imaxtree. Still Lifes: J Muckle/Studio D.

Page 186: Main Photos (from left): Olivia Graham; Imaxtree. Still Lifes (clockwise from top left): Jesus Ayala/Studio D; J Muckle/Studio D; J Muckle/Studio D.

Page 187: Main Photos (clockwise from top left): Sara Silver; Chris Eckert/Studio D (2). Still Lifes (clockwise from top right): Jesus Ayala/Studio D; J Muckle/Studio D.

Page 188: J Muckle/Studio D.

Page 189: J Muckle/Studio D (top left). Jesus Ayala/Studio D (bottom right).

Page 190: J Muckle/Studio D.

Page 191: J Muckle/Studio D (bottom left). Christopher Coppola/Studio D (top right).

THIS BOOK WAS PRODUCED BY

powerHouse Packaging & Supply, Inc.
37 Main Street
Brooklyn, NY 11201
www.powerHousePackaging.com

Publisher Sharyn Rosart

Creative Director Lynne Yeamans

Writer Baze Mpinja
Photo Editor Joslyn Blair Winkfield
Copy Editor Emmy Favilla

SEVENTEEN THANK-YOUS

Joanna Saltz, Jessica Musumeci, Alison Jurado, Yesenia Almonte,
Molly Ritterbeck, Joslyn Winkfield, Baze Mpinja, Jasmine Snow, Carissa Rosenberg,
Marisa Carroll, Emmy Favilla, Robert Gillo, and Jacqueline Deval

Chris Navratil, Craig Herman, Frances Soo Ping Chow, Cindy De La Hoz,
and the whole Running Press team

Sharyn Rosart, Lynne Yeamans, and the entire powerHouse team

POWERHOUSE PACKAGING & SUPPLY THANK-YOUS

Chris Navratil, Frances Soo Ping Chow, Cindy De La Hoz, and everyone at Running Press

Ann Shoket, Joanna Saltz, Jessica Musumeci, Yesenia Almonte,
Sally Abbey, Alison Jurado, and everyone at *Seventeen*

Baze Mpinja, Joslyn B. Winkfield, Emmy Favilla, Lana Le, Stephen Singerman,
and everyone who assisted in the creation of this book